to see what you do
with all you are.
with love.
Denise

Issues
in Your
Tissues

Heal Body and Emotion
from the Inside Out

Denise LaBarre, L.M.T.

 Healing Catalyst Press

Illustration: Paul Tatum, www.paultatum.com
Book Design: Patricia Rasch, www.bookandcoverdesign.com
Author photo: Aubrey Hord, www.aubreyhord.com

For Additional copies of this book and more information, go to:
www.healingcatalyst.com

or write:
Healing Catalyst Press
P.O. Box 695
Haiku, HI 96708

ISBN: 978-0-9824772-0-5

Disclaimer: This book is not intended as a substitute for the advice of a physician or psychologist. Readers who have any medical or psychiatric problems that would contraindicate them should not attempt the exercises presented here.

This book contains references to actual sessions and conversations the author has had with real people. However, names and identifying information have been changed to protect the privacy of those involved.

For Audrey,
my mom and role model
for unconditional love

Thanks are in order to many people for their help and support with this book – most notably: Paul Tatum, Pat Rasch, Georgia Hughes, Roan and Susana Browne, Otto Pozzo, Deborah Iida, Lea, Adam, and Mike Lundblad. As this book makes its way in the world, this list will grow.

Thank you, too.

Contents

The greatest work of your life is to re-member *and integrate all aspects of yourself.*

Introduction

Welcome. I'm glad you are here.

First of all, I'd like to acknowledge the miracle that is your body. It gives you pleasure, heals wounds, accomplishes heroic feats, and works hard through abuse and neglect. Your body always does its very best given the conditions it faces and constantly tells you what it needs to be healthy. It loves you. I know this because thousands of bodies have told me that's what bodies do. No matter what condition it's in, your body deserves love and respect.

Early in my life, I began doing bodywork in response to distress I intuitively felt in people I loved. I found I could feel stuck emotional energy and that it is often at the root of physical symptoms. I learned to translate the body's language of tension and pain into messages the mind could use to feel better. Over years of making connections with people of all ages and backgrounds, I saw that we share the same basic pattern. We are born with our minds and bodies in seamless communication and our emotions pass through us without resistance. But we soon learn to stuff down "unacceptable" emotion and ignore our body's natural guidance as we become socialized. We shut down parts of ourselves to survive trauma but often don't open back up. We come to live primarily in our minds, breathe minimally, and push our bodies past healthy limits into stress and dis-ease. It doesn't need to be that way though. Our bodies are ever ready to heal.

I'd love to help you feel more vibrant and healthy in your body. With your permission, I will guide you inside to deepen your breath, release held emotion, and reconnect your vital energy. My approach is intuitive, grounded, and playful; the work is simple. I re-mind you to listen to your body and make the connections for yourself. You already know how to do it but you may need some encouragement to take action. I wrote this book to share my insights and give you that encouragement. May it be a catalyst for your greater well-being.

My life has given me a handy set of tools to do this work. I was separated from my mother at birth, which made me develop the intuitive antennae common to people who survive deep, early trauma. I also make use of an attribute called "clairsentience," the ability to sense underlying emotion. A clairsentient person can sense the deep sadness behind a smile or can feel the underlying mood in a gathering of people. Many people have this ability, and of course, some more than others. Like musical ability, it needs to be developed and exercised to become strong and accurate. I have developed this ability to the degree that I am now called an emotional intuitive.

When I was seven years old, I looked at my overweight, over-worked, stressed-out, social worker mom and thought, "If somebody doesn't help her body, she's not going to make it." It was as if I heard her body calling for help. So I began massaging her regularly, 2-3 times a week. I'd have her lie face down on her bed, sit astride her hips, and do what I could to rub away the tension in her shoulders, neck and back. My hands were small, my reach was short; but in my mind, I'd encourage her body, thinking things like, I know she doesn't exercise or eat right and she neglects you. Please keep her going, Body. Please don't give up on her. Don't die. With practice, and because I loved her so much, I learned to feel subtle changes in her muscles and the energy that flowed through her body. I didn't judge her obesity; I was simply grateful to her body for carrying my mom through so much stress and neglect.

As I grew up, my mom always talked about feelings and people's psychological motivations for behaving the way they do. I began reading her graduate school psychology textbooks when I was eleven. I plowed through Freud and Jung and the popular psychology books on our bookshelves. Then when I'd exhausted our library, I read more psychology books from the public library. When I studied anatomy in high school I started to connect the dots – seeing how body, emotion and mind are interconnected. By the time I left for college, I was thoroughly steeped in and using the concepts of modern psychology, connecting the physical dots, and constantly gathering more information.

Meanwhile, I racked up hands-on experience massaging people. Whenever someone mentioned an ache or pain and would let me, I would massage them. I found I could "hear" what other bodies were saying, not just my mom's. It's fascinating. My yearbooks are full of comments like: "Thanks for all the great massages." "Thanks for fixing my neck that time." "Don't stop using those great hands." It was simply something I did naturally. After college while I was managing a translation and interpretation agency, I decided to go to massage school. Since then, I have worked on and learned from thousands of bodies as a professional massage therapist. I am constantly watching and learning from athletes, from my own experiences, from other people's experiences. I am fascinated with people, their bodies and their psychology. I ask questions and connect ideas and learn from everything I do. The human body constantly amazes me!

On my own healing journey, I found that when I got standard massages, I didn't release my deeply-held physical tension. When I went through conventional psychological counseling, again, I didn't release my deeply-held emotions. In the 1980s the idea that mind and body are part of an energetic continuum began to penetrate the general culture and filtered into individual healing practices. I found massage experiences where I could talk with the bodyworker about energy she felt in my body and get insightful feedback and my body started to release at deeper levels. When I found a counselor who used play and intuition to access my old emotional wounds, they began to heal. I found through direct experience that my body, mind and emotions all had to be engaged for deep healing to happen.

Over the years, asking questions and making connections for myself, my work developed beyond standard massage therapy into something more. I grew adept at intuitively feeling emotional energy held in muscle tissue and translating that into concepts my clients could understand and use to release their pent-up energy. I have always loved learning languages. I love the different sounds and it excites me to connect ideas I only have direct access to in a "foreign" tongue. It wasn't much of a stretch to realize I was hearing the language of the human body and translating it for minds that had gotten out of the habit of listening. In a way I became a "body-mind translator."

I saw that full breathing is the key to releasing physical tension and the emotional energy that often accompanies it. I found that even when a person wants to breathe more or deeper, he rarely knows how - even though proper breathing is ancient wisdom. So I developed a simple, quick way to teach people to breathe deeply. I learned how to speak to the mind, saying just enough so it understands why it might want to release its habitual stranglehold and let the lungs expand all the way. When the body experiences how much better it feels to breathe into tension rather than clench into it, it relaxes, space opens up and healing energy flows through it. The way I see it, if I give a man a massage, I can relax him for a day. If I teach him to breathe and make his own inner connections, I can relax him for a lifetime.

It was a natural progression to use my background in psychology and my intuitive strength to help people connect the physical symptoms they experienced with the emotional energy they carry. I found I kept saying the same things to very different people. Doctors and hairdressers, teachers and police officers – regardless of education or life-experience, people didn't know how to help themselves feel better because they hadn't made the connections between physical symptom and energetic cause. When people feel how minimal breathing, stress, stuffing down emotions, and physical problems are connected in their bodies and experience the shift to full breathing and release, they get excited and see more possibilities for improvement.

Once people begin to make these connections, the results they get are remarkably similar. At the minimum, their breathing opens up and they feel better. Their eyes shine brighter and clearer, they look and feel younger and more relaxed, and they find greater ease, aliveness and space in their bodies. I remember one super-tight man who enthusiastically dove into opening his breathing. When he got up, I told him that he looked ten years younger. He told me, "I feel thirty years younger!" When a person is willing, making those inner connections can result in fabulous, life-changing shifts. Tumors disappear, decades-old grudges are forgiven, and the body-mind transforms itself.

I often use stories as a healing tool. I find that telling a quick story about someone with a similar issue is a gentle, effective way to show clients they are not alone and give them permission and encouragement to explore their own issues. The stories translate what the body says into intuitive concepts the mind can work with. Some stories I tell frequently, others I bring out only occasionally. Before I begin a session I don't know if I will use any stories at all - many sessions are mostly wordless. When I do get an idea to tell a story, it's usually in response to a problem or concern a client mentions. I check in intuitively to make sure it's appropriate to tell and then continue to check in with the client (verbally or non-verbally) as I go.

The stories I've included here are the ones that have helped people most often. They are distilled versions of actual body-work sessions that leave out the non-verbal communication and silences that happen in real time but don't serve in the re-telling. The people in them are just like you and me. Their inner heroes shine forth as they are willing to explore uncharted territory in their own bodies and emotional experience. And who doesn't like to hear stories they can relate to?

So step into my world for a little while. Listen to some stories and let them entertain and inspire you. Fill your lungs and effortlessly breathe in the transitions throughout your day. Make the connection between the tension you feel in your body and the unresolved emotions you carry. Rediscover the ease and space you had in your body when you were a child. It's easier than you think.

There's emotional treasure inside you and I want to help you reclaim it. You only have to be willing to explore the energetic space inside your body – out of your mind, below the neck. You don't have to know how already. I'll show you the way. I am now asking your mind for permission to enter. Without it the door is barred. If you will read on with an open mind, and do the inner work, I promise you will get something out of the process. Let's see what we can do together if you give yourself permission to come alive inside!

The book you have in your hands is an invitation for you to make the mind-body connection for yourself. The approach is straightforward and body-centered. With your cooperation, we can make the same connections in your mind and body that I have made with my hands-on clients.

In the pages to come, I'm going to discuss the following ideas:

- Growing up, we face situations that emotionally overwhelmed us. We learned to stuff down uncomfortable feelings in our bodies and hold them there with minimal breathing. Over time, shallow breathing became our normal habit.

- We come to live "in our minds", run by obsessive thinking and largely cut off from the innate joy and juiciness in our bodies.

- Unfelt, unprocessed emotional energy accumulates and we experience it as pain or disease. (Read that word as dis-ease.) Pain and dis-ease are the body's way of telling us that we have reached overload. They are our call to heal.

- Along with the "negative" emotions such as sadness and anger that we carry in our bodies there are joy, expansiveness and creativity that got shut off in the same process.

- Releasing long-held emotion doesn't have to be difficult, scary or harsh; in fact, it can be quick and easy. It can be as gentle as a sigh or as electric as an orgasm. The release creates space to expand into your bigger, whole self. It also feels a lot better not to carry that energy around anymore!

- Full breathing initiates the flow of healing energy. Once you feel the difference between clenching into tension and breathing into it, you can open the flow of energy and begin healing on physical, emotional, mental, and/ or spiritual levels. We will be exploring the physical and emotional levels here.

- You can't just read the words. You have to take action if you want results. Healing happens as you put these ideas into practice.

Whether or not these ideas are new to you, my goal is to help you see them from a perspective you haven't seen before, give you simple tools to help you reconnect with your body, and the inspiration to use them to feel better.

A note on navigating this book

This book addresses several different levels of experience and depicts people at very different stages of their healing process. Please do not feel that you have to read it straight through. I recommend looking at the table of contents to see where your intuition guides you and begin reading there. That's good practice trusting your intuition – which is part of the opening I'm talking about. Think of the stories as keys that unlock intuitive understanding. You may be ready for the insights from some of the stories but not others. You certainly don't need all of them at once. But since you are already reading this, I'd bet that there is something of value for you here.

Also consider picking up this book again in a few weeks or months to see what jumps out at you after you've digested some of the stories. Intuitive powers, like every other, need to be exercised; they will grow as you use them. You are learning and evolving, and an idea that you might not be able to digest now might be just what you're ready to hear down the road.

I wish you the very best on your healing journey.

All my love,

Denise

CHAPTER 1 —

Breathing Like You Mean It

The Important Things (in order):
The Thoughts we think
The Air we breathe
The Water we drink
The Exercise we get
The Food we eat

~ Yogi Bajhan

Breathing—our most fundamental ability—is so critical to our well-being that if we go without it for even three minutes, we die. Yet almost every adult I meet breathes shallowly as a regular habit. That's where stress begins. On the table when I ask clients to show me their biggest breath, they can't fill their lungs all the way. My clients tell me they know they need to breathe more or better but the intention gets buried in the turmoil of their hectic daily lives. They walk around under-oxygenated and breath-less, which is the foundation for all major disease and stress-related disorders.

It doesn't have to be that way—for them, or you.

If you could improve your breathing without changing your schedule at all, would you do it? What if it doesn't cost anything and you can do it any time without interrupting your day or anyone knowing you're doing it? What if in breathing more, you could gradually clean out your whole system and over time, ease symptoms of allergies, high blood pressure, overeating, smoking, and stress out of your body? What if you could release the old emotional baggage you've carried for years and find ease and joy in your body? Well, you *can* do all those things and this book will show you how.

That's just Chapter One. After that, I will show you what your body has been saying to you for years, trying to get your attention with pain and other symptoms. I want to serve as your body's interpreter, translating the physical sensations and signals you may have a habit of ignoring into thoughts and ideas you can work with. I give you this information through stories that your intuition will recognize as containing truth. There's a lot here. I will give your mind enough to chew on so it will get out of the way and let your intuition guide you to greater healing.

The process starts with your willingness to take a full breath. Healing change happens as you breathe more fully and let oxygen and energy flow through your body. With each breath you open and feel better rather than shut down and feel worse. First, you have to decide that you want to make a change. Then you need to feel that you *can* make that change. What I have to show you about fuller breathing is so simple and so easy to do that once you get it, you're going to want to play with it. And that play will feel great. There are even greater treasures to discover within your inner landscape if you are willing to explore further. You already have the answers to what's ailing you. Your body has been telling you all along. Here's your opportunity to learn your body's language

Full breath is our natural birthright. We are designed to breathe using the abdominal muscles and diaphragm to pump air and energy in and out of the lungs. That's how babies breathe—from the belly. Unfortunately the habit of breathing fully and deeply usually shifts to shallow breathing as the pressures of socialization and stressful or scary experiences drive us out of our body and "into our head."

We don't even realize it's happening. Our breathing changes automatically in response to perceived threats and to anything we resist—i.e. stress. That's part of the "fight or flight" response, which we will explore further in Chapter 5. It's a survival mechanism we overuse and then we develop the unconscious habit of breathing less in order not to feel emotions the mind says are too scary or overwhelming. Some of us started out in an unwelcoming womb and felt we were fighting for our lives. For many, the shut-down happened in childhood, during the course of socialization. We felt emotions like anger, fear, rejection, sadness, and frustration, acted them out, and then got in trouble for it. We then learned to stuff down those emotions by holding or limiting our breath. We buried the yucky feelings deep in our bodies and continued accumulating more.

Even if we didn't have a scary childhood, we may have adopted the habit of "sucking in the gut" to look thinner. We found that if we held in our tummy muscles and breathed shallowly, the tummy stayed flatter and we didn't look babyish or "fat" anymore.

We weren't trying to limit your breath *per se,* but that was the net effect. Over time, shallow breathing became "normal."

As adults, we find ourselves thinking too much, breathing too little, and wanting relief from stress. The mind is in control and it does everything it can to stay that way. It becomes a tyrant that hoards our energy up in the head and out of the body. It won't let us relax completely, won't let the energy circulate through the body so we don't *feel* the unwanted feelings stored there.

When we think, we pull energy up from our body, lock it up there with tight neck and shoulder muscles, and breathe minimally or hold our breath as we concentrate. This drains the body of its energy as the energy accumulates in the head area. When we do this all day long, by quitting time, we feel out of balance and too tired to have fun in the evening. We might recognize that we need to breathe more but life is busy, full of stress, and we don't see when or how we can work on our breathing.

Breathing fully, the way we were born to do, circulates energy through the body, revitalizing and nourishing all systems. As we deepen the breath, our muscles relax, thinking slows, and we feel more space in our bodies. We invite creativity to flow through. The mind looses its stranglehold on our attention and allows us to feel our emotions. The mind tells us that feeling all our undigested emotions will overwhelm—even kill—us. But that's not so.

Think of it like reopening a dammed waterway. Once you understand what's involved and get a little practice with the valves (your breathing) you can let a bit through at a time. The stories here are meant to help you understand the waterways and some of the damming mechanisms. There might be an initial rush at the outset but once that pent-up water starts moving, the water flows naturally without doing damage. We can open the emotional floodgates gradually by practicing with our breath so there's no violent flood.

Your emotions are a fabulous part of being human and when you allow them to be a part of you, you feel alive and wonderful. You have a fantastic capacity for joy. You have incredible insight and aliveness in your body if you allow your attention back in there enough to experience it. Reconnecting with your emotions is a vital part of healing. Your soul knows it. Your body knows it too. You just have to remember yourself (read that as re-member) and come back to the connectedness you were born to live. I believe it is the fundamental work of a human lifetime to heal and re-integrate the body, emotions, mind, and spirit. And each person must do it for him- or herself. No one can do it for you. It starts by taking a full breath. So, if you are willing, let's jump in. Let's start by opening your breathing and see what develops from there.

I propose to show you how to breathe fully, for the rest of your life without taking classes or shifting your daily schedule at all. If you are ready for that, read on. I'd like to show your mind what it looks like so it doesn't block the process. Then you simply have to try it. If that sounds a bit scary to you, skip to Chapter 2 and read until you want to come back and learn to open your breathing.

As a warm-up, start by picturing the energy in your body as a circuit. When you think, you pull energy into your head area. Imagine sucking energy up through your neck and into your head as if your neck were a straw. Then you hold that energy up in your head by tightening your neck and shoulder muscles. Now, take a couple of deep breaths. Breathe like this until you feel energy flow down into and around your body. (I mean it, put the book down now and breathe. Look for this to mark your place.)

Once your energy is flowing down and through your body, think about something that worries you, or multiply 310 times 22. Then feel inside your body. Did you feel energy move upward into your head? Now take another few slow deep breaths. (Yes, now. Put the book down.) Did you feel the energy flow back down into your body when you breathed again? Play with this feeling until you get it, until you feel energy moving as you direct it, up with your thoughts, down into the body.

Now to give you a more detailed picture of the process I use, I'm going to tell you a story about a man so locked up in his armored body he could barely breathe.

Terminator Man

I would describe Harden as an alpha male,[1] in his late forties, 6′4″ tall, and weighing about 300 lbs. He came to Maui as head of a marketing conference. I asked him if he had played football. He grunted, "Yeah, a hundred pounds ago." He told me he gets a massage fairly regularly. Before he lay down on the table, he looked down at all 5′2″ of me with an expression

---

1   The "alpha" is the dominant member of an animal group and is usually highly intelligent and aggressive.

that said, "Go ahead Honey, give it your best shot."

His was the epitome of a body heavily-clad with what I call "body armor." Such a person is ready to take on anything and anyone at any time. His conscious awareness stays in his mind while his body must constantly follow the mind's orders to brace up, overcome, and play the strong one. He unconsciously responds to the constant challenges and emotional pain in his life by sealing himself behind the energetic armor in his muscles and then adding layers of emotional energy-storing fat on top of that. The pattern becomes so all-encompassing and heavy that he doesn't know where to begin if he wants to change it. When I meet this kind of body, I feel for an opening. I want to let him know I'm on his side. I don't want to take him on in any kind of battle. Lord knows he'd win. My intention is to help loosen that defensive armoring if he will allow it [See Aesop's Sun and Wind story in Chapter 9].

As I started working on Harden's back, I felt his muscles closing, like plates of special-effects armor snapping shut in a science fiction movie. It was not so much a physical movement as an energetic effect. I was so startled at the strength of my impression of armored plates snapping shut that I bypassed my usual spiel about breathing and went right to the core of it. I sensed that Harden sincerely wanted relief from all the tension he hauled around—armor is heavy, after all—but he had no idea about how to unbuckle it and take it off. I checked in intuitively to see if I should say something to him about what I was feeling in his body. I got a 'yes'.

I stopped working but kept contact and explained, "I just felt the muscles in your back close off to me. Have you seen the Terminator movies?" He had. "You know those overlapping metal plates that close off like a camera diaphragm?" I made the motion with my hands on his back. He nodded. "Look at you, then look at me. You're three times as big as I am. There's no way I'm going to muscle you into relaxing. You win. If you don't allow me in there, I could work my hands to a bloody pulp and you'd be just as tight and uncomfortable as you are now. If you want me to help you, you have to open the door and let me in. If you are willing to take some deep breaths and let your guard down, I promise I won't hurt you." I don't think people usually spoke to him like this.

"What do I have to do?" he asked.

"Breathe. Can I teach you?"

"Go for it."

My guess is that my intention to respect his defenses, expressed directly, appealed to his will like bowing to a king before asking for his help in a campaign. I asked him to breathe into his belly, to let the energy extend down to his toes. I told him about taking the time to fill his lungs from the bottom up, like sand filling a bucket.

With each breath it felt as if the armor plates relaxed a bit. His muscles began to soften and the work had some effect. When he turned over, I saw that his breath still reached about mid-chest.

I put his hand on his belly. "Here. See if you can breathe all the way down here. Make your hand move up and down." He pulled in some air but his belly didn't expand. "You know when you were a little kid and said, "Look Mom, I'm fat!" and you stuck out your belly?" He smiled with a little nod. "Try that now."

He pushed out his belly about half way. "Now breathe in." He sucked in his belly and breathed into his chest. "That's the opposite. That's your old habit. Try gently puffing out your belly and then inhaling." He puffed and exhaled. "Try it again. Don't worry about letting your belly move out. Your guts have to get out of the way so your lungs can expand downward and fill from the bottom up." He tried again. "See if you can hold your belly out and inhale while it's still big." This time he pulled in a little air. "That's it! More of that. You want to use your abdominal muscles like a bellows. They expand when you inhale, squeeze to exhale."

I put my hand on my own belly and breathed with him to demonstrate. "See? This is how babies are born breathing. This is how you used to breathe before you were socialized. It often shuts down around kindergarten." He was getting it but still didn't exhale completely. "Use your abdominal muscles to push out the air. The exhale is like squeezing a tube of toothpaste, from the bottom up." He was working too hard. "Okay, relax. That's great. That's a lot all at once. See if you can gently and gradually let your lungs expand."

I continued massaging his legs while he played with the sensations of a full breath. I occasionally encouraged him or gave him a prompt. He was breathing more deeply than when we started.

I told him, "You can train yourself to take a full breath during the *transitions* in your day. When you're on a tense phone call or driving through tight traffic, you're not going to be breathing deeply. Your mind will be hoarding the energy—and rightfully so. But afterward, when you put the phone down, when you're stopped at a stoplight, *that's* when you throw your belly out to start breathing deeply again. It's like pushing the reset button." As his mind thought about this, I could feel his body relaxing and his breath deepening.

"Breathe anytime you're waiting—at the doctor's office, at the airport, waiting for your wife to get dressed, during dull meetings. When I get into my car and have my hand on the door handle, I tell myself, *Okay Denise, you're driving now.* No matter what I've been amping out about, rushing to get ready, I throw out my belly and breathe. I'm a better driver when I do—more present and in my body.

"Harden, this is an old habit you're looking to shift. You clearly want to feel better. It can't be easy living in a body with that much defensive tension."

"You got that right," he said.

"For the rest of the day, see how many times you can catch yourself not breathing or breathing shallowly. Don't beat yourself up about it—just notice, throw out your belly, and deepen your breath. Then keep breathing. At night, as you're lying there in bed, take ten slow, deep breaths. At first your mind won't want to let go. It'll want to hog the energy. But keep at it, slowly and deliberately. By about the fourth breath, if you've really let your lungs expand, your mind will start to say, "Okay, maybe I can let that go until the morning." And keep breathing. I promise you'll sleep better without all that energy stuck up in your head."

We talked about the importance of breath and oxygen to let the muscles relax and about how his mind has to see the benefit of letting down his defenses and allow it to happen.

"Thank you," he said. "No one's ever told me any of this stuff before."

"Well, maybe not in this way. It's so simple. The mind loves to make things complicated. The only challenging part is remembering to practice when everything else crowds in. But the more you do it, the easier it gets."

When he got up from the table he didn't look like he was about to block a tackle anymore and he stood more at ease. He played with taking belly breaths in a standing position. He clearly had the idea and was working with it.

I told him, "You don't have to stick your belly out that far every time," I said. "But now, when you're learning it, it helps to exaggerate to open and get the feel of it. You haven't suddenly gained any weight, after all. You're just filling your lungs with air. Practice when you're relaxed and eventually you'll be able to do it under fire as well."

"Wow," he tussled his hair. "That was the best massage I've ever had." He swung his arms and twisted his hips, testing how his body felt.

"I'm glad," I said. "That's because you opened your breathing and let it in. From now on, when you get a massage, even if the therapist doesn't remind you to breathe, make sure you do it for yourself." He grinned and nodded.

Harden still had a lot of long-held energy stuck in his muscles but he had finally penetrated his own defenses. His mind had allowed his awareness back into his body—and he could *feel* how much better his body felt when that happened. He could build upon that experience and go further with it, practicing breathing deeply during his daily life.

Locking energy up above the neck and breathing minimally can be a self-perpetuating spiral. The more you pull energy into your head to think, the less energy you have in your body. The mental voice gets louder and continually drowns out the physical voice, which gets weaker. Your mind begins to manage your body rather than the other way around. At the end of a busy day—a day of thinking too much and being driven by your mind—your body feels drained (it is drained, just *upward*); your neck and shoulders feel as tight as a drum; and your head feels like it's going to explode. It can feel like it's full of angry bees. If that sounds familiar it's because your mind has hogged your energy all day. To prevent that and finish the day with some energy left to enjoy your evening, you have to breathe *in the transitions*, the time in-between important tasks. Read on, I'll tell you how.

 If you think of the breath-energy as water and your head area (mental body) and physical body as two cups, you want the energy to flow continually back and forth between them. If you keep pouring the water into your head all day, eventually your head's cup will be full and tight—even overflowing—and your body's cup will be empty. The cycle cannot continue this way. You want to pour energy back into the body so the cycle can continue. You do this by taking a full, deep breath. As you breathe fully and pour energy out of your head and back into your body, you can almost feel the angry bees relax as they get more space to move around.

Fortunately, even if you have a deeply ingrained habit of breathing shallowly you can reset your breathing pattern any time you like. It may take dedicated practice but the process is simple once you understand what you've been doing and how to shift it.

Now take a second to think about your lungs. The lungs are shaped roughly like triangles with the majority of their capacity in the bottom half. If you only allow your chest to expand as you breathe, you are only getting air into the top part and you are shorting yourself 50–80 percent of the oxygen your lungs were meant to take in with each breath[2]. *[Fig. 1.1]* Multiply this subtle, constant, and critical oxygen deprivation over a lifetime and you can see how it might impact your health.

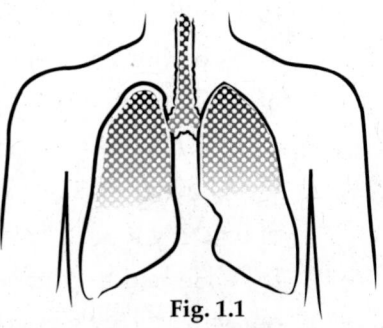

Fig. 1.1

The solution is to take a full breath, the way trained singers and yogis and horn players do. You do this by breathing into your belly, the way you were designed to do. Throw out your belly and let your lungs fill from the bottom up. *[Fig. 1.2]* Your lungs are shaped like big triangles with the majority of their capacity at the bottom and it takes a few beats to fill them all the way. If you try it and your chest expands first, keep playing with this process, expanding lower. Think, "belly breath."

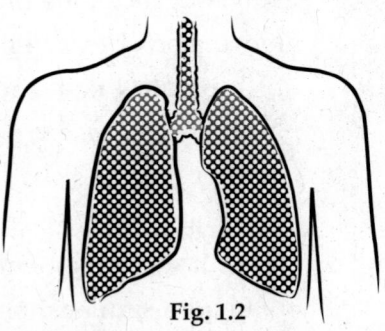

Fig. 1.2

I remember a man who seemed eager to breathe fully but his body was not used to taking a full breath. When he had trouble taking a full breath, I said to him, "You know how when you blow up a balloon and let the air out, the sides stick

2   Hendricks, Gay, *Conscious Breathing: Breathwork for Health, Stress Relief and Personal Growth*. (Bantam, 1995).

together? Then you have to blow even harder to unstick the sides before you can blow up the balloon again? Well, think of your lungs like balloons with the sides and bottom stuck shut. When you go to fill your lungs, you may have to push a little harder at first to open where it's gotten stuck from lack of use. Try it now." He did. I could tell it felt strange to him at first. He had to practice letting his abdominal muscles move outward. "That's great," I said. "Let your belly expand, like a kid having fun. He was wearing pants that pinched his belly and I suggested he undo the top button so his tummy could move. Each breath he took got a little deeper. By about the fifth breath I could feel energy starting to flow down into his body. His face broke into a huge, sweet smile and said, "I haven't breathed that way in a looong time!" I got a flash of what he must have looked like as a small boy—radiant and alive. It was a moment of pure joy.

I had a similar moment with a stressed-out, energetically bound-up businessman. About thirty minutes into the treatment he was breathing fully and clearly enjoying himself. He told me, "Last month I was away on a business trip and feeling terrible. I tried going into one of those oxygen bars[3]. I tell you, I felt so much better after that. But you know what? I think this feels even better." When he got up from the treatment, he shook my hand saying, "You just saved me a whole lot of money. I was planning to buy an oxygen machine for my house."

---

3   An oxygen bar sells time to breathe concentrated oxygen from tanks—like the ones emphysema patients often use. Depending on your state of health, the oxygen can give you a big lift toward feeling well. The more under-oxygenated you are, the greater the difference you feel with the extra oxygen.

I laughed. "You don't need an expensive machine. You already have all the equipment you need. And it's free. You just have to use it."

Now, Dear Reader, let's see what we can do with your breathing. Read the exercise through and then set yourself up with at least ten, private, uninterrupted minutes to do it. If you can't take the opportunity now, read the exercise through and come back to do it as soon as you can.

EXERCISE 1: Breathing Like you Mean it

1.   Lie down comfortably so that you can concentrate on the internal feelings without having to hold yourself up. If you're wearing anything tight across your belly, loosen it so you can really puff your belly out. Now take a full breath, as big as you can to fill your lungs. Do it again. Close your eyes and feel it from inside.

How did that feel? Did your chest rise? If so, you can probably go deeper. Keep doing this and feel your breath deepen.

2.   This time as you breathe in, think of pulling in breath and energy all the way down to your toes. Put your hand on your belly to make sure it's expanding with the in-breath. Remember playing as a little kid, puffing out your belly, and saying, "Look Mom, I'm fat!" Kids love to play with what their bodies can do. See if you can puff your belly out like that in order to reactivate deeper breathing. You're not gaining any weight, after all, you're just breathing. See if you can let the little kid in you giggle at how that feels and let your lungs simply and gently fill with air from the bottom up. Keep at it until it feels like your belly is open and relaxed and you can fill your lungs all the way.

Many adults have trouble doing this because they've habitually held in their bellies for years. When I was re-learning to breathe fully, it took me *three days* of constant trying to get my belly muscles to release enough that I could fill my lungs fully. If you have a deep-seated habit of sucking in your gut to look thinner or to avoid fearful feelings held in the belly area, it may take more practice to get comfortable with this. Don't worry about it. The point is not that you have to stick your belly way out to breath fully but you do have to engage your diaphragm and belly muscles, and you can't do that if you're holding them in. The more you do it, the easier it becomes and the better it feels. Try it again now.

3. Once you can expand your belly all the way, breathe in gently and fully and hold your lungs full for a beat or two. Get used to the sensation of allowing life-giving oxygen and energy into your body, of being full. You may get a feeling of wonder and expansion. You also might feel a little light-headed so it's best to start out doing this while lying down. Breathing this deeply allows in more oxygen than the body may be used to. Be gentle and encouraging with yourself. You're simply doing what you are designed to do—breathe fully. It could feel scary if your mind has fought for a long time to keep your consciousness away from deeply-held feelings. If so, tell yourself you're just breathing, no need to battle demons right now. Continue as long as you are comfortable, then stop.

4.   Explore the exhalation. You can't breathe in fully if your lungs are still partly full of used air. Use your abdominal muscles to squeeze out air on the exhale. Your belly muscles and diaphragm are designed to do the work of emptying and filling your lungs and that includes a gentle contraction as you breathe out. Play with it until you can exhale as long as you inhale. Breathing out is just as important as breathing in.

5.   Remember your breathing as often as you can. When you catch yourself breathing shallowly, don't scold yourself for not breathing, simply throw out your belly and take a full breath. Then resume whatever you were doing. That's one more deep breath you wouldn't have taken if you hadn't noticed.

6.   Today, see if you can catch yourself breathing shallowly three times by the time you go to bed. When you catch yourself, don't scold yourself for not breathing. Just notice, and say *Isn't that interesting? There's that habit.*—And then take a deep breath. Every time you catch yourself and breathe, that's one more deep breath than you would have taken otherwise. If you get stuck trying too hard, simply think, *belly breath* and your body will know to relax and let your diaphragm fill your lungs. Tomorrow, see if you can catch yourself not breathing five times—and breathe each time, in and out. That's five more deep breaths, five more lung-fulls of oxygen you have given yourself than you would not have otherwise. The next day try to catch yourself ten times, and keep going. If you slack off for a day or two, don't fret, just resume as soon as you catch yourself again. Retraining an old habit takes persistence.

7. You can continue to expand your practice by breathing in the transitions of your day. You can also take five minutes to do deep or counted breathing once or twice in your day. There are many ways to expand your breathing. Start slowly and build on what's comfortable. Just do it.

8. Breathing fully is a great remedy for anxiety, stress, and bad feelings in general. If you wake up in the middle of the night and want to get back to sleep, throw your belly out and take slow, full breaths, making sure you exhale fully. This will calm your mind, you will rest better even if you don't fall back to sleep. Decide and remember to throw out your belly and deepen your breath any time you feel resistance to what's going on around you.

Advanced level: Counted breathing. Throughout the ages, humans have used counted breathing practices to expand their concentration and inner awareness. Counting beats while you breathe keeps the mind occupied and the breath steady. A beat can be taken as one heart beat or one second but the point is the *ratio* of time spent inhaling, exhaling and holding, not the speed. The focus is on quality not quantity so six fast beats are not necessarily better than four slow, even ones. If you are already comfortable with belly breathing, you may want to try a counted breath to deepen your breathing practice.

I do what I call "square breathing" because it makes sense to me to balance each of the four parts of the breath equally and I like how it feels. I first met this pattern in a yoga class and got frustrated when I couldn't manage the eight slow beats the instructor counted out. Then I realized it's simply a lengthened 1:1:1:1 ratio pattern and re-timed it to work for me. I started out with a four-beat square and have gradually increased the dura-tion of each "side." If I neglect my practice for a while, I go back to four beats and start building again from there.

Square breathing. Start by exhaling fully and slowly. Gently squeeze your belly mus-cles to push a little more air out of the lungs. Don't strain. Then breathe in for two beats, hold the breath for two beats, exhale for two beats, and hold the belly and lungs empty for two beats.

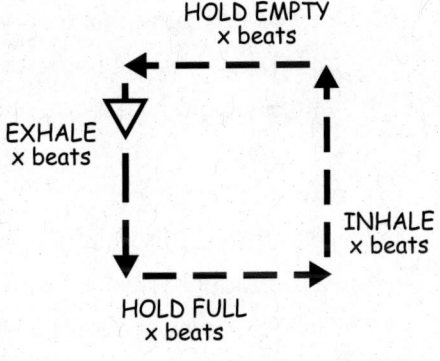

Repeat. It will take a few "squares" for the breath to settle and even out. If two beats feels too short, gradually lengthen the sides until it feels right. Once you get the squares even, see if you can continue for five minutes or at least twelve breaths. Don't do more than you are comfortable with. You can start with three or six beats—you will find your comfort level pretty quickly. If you have never done this kind of thing before, be patient with yourself. Start gently and work up to as many beats per side as feels good. Do this for five minutes per session and see where you take it from there. Bedtime is a great time to practice.

There are many advanced breathing patterns out there, each with its own esoteric merits. Some patterns emphasize either the inhalation or the exhalation, or leave out either the full hold or empty hold. Inhalation builds energy and exhalation dissipates it. So keep in mind that if one phase is proportionally longer or more vigorous, it is emphasized. Advanced breathing practices can have a powerful calming or enervating effect in the body, and like anything that has power, what might be good for one person might not be good for another. For example, holding the breath for several beats after inhalation is great for building energy but is contraindicated for high blood pressure. Don't do anything that feels wrong for you or push yourself too far. Take on what feels right to you and build gradually. Keep it simple enough that you stick with it. Just get started.

Breathing fully may feel strange at first but as you practice it will gradually feel normal and you'll feel really great doing it. It took time for your habit of shallow breathing to get that entrenched and it will take time and practice to deepen it. Each time you notice yourself breathing shallowly, say to yourself, "Great, another opportunity to shift the habit. Breathe from the belly." Once you have that down, you can try to breathe deeply in stressful situations. I started training myself to take a deep breath before I intervene if my kids' arguing escalates. Then I noticed

I EXPECTED OUR TEACHER TO BE A LITTLE OLDER

magic happening. More often than not now, I wind up not feeling the need to intervene at all and they settle it themselves.

The next chance you get, watch a healthy infant breathe. You will see the belly puffing out and the little toes and fingers moving as the energy flows in. You will be watching a natural master. Feel free to be inspired and instructed.

Sometimes it helps to picture your breath as life-giving water and your body as the garden. If you don't breath fully, your garden is parched. It's not something you do once and then you're finished. A garden needs water continually; your body needs full breath-energy, again and again, every so-many seconds. Give yourself that drink of energy. Water your garden.

People ask me if it's better to breathe through the nose or mouth. For our purposes here, any way you can breathe fully is great. Refinements can come later. When I first learned this, I breathed through my mouth because my nose and sinuses were usually congested. As my sinuses cleared, I began to take in breath through my nose. The goal is simply a deep, full breath. Do what works for you.

If you haven't done the breathing exercise yet, mark this page and come back to it when you have the chance. No more reading until you do it. Everything else in the book will make better sense if you can open your breathing and feel inside your body.

Breathing in the Transitions

Breathing fully is not something you do when you're finished with all your other work. You need to do it throughout your day. You can do it *in between* tasks, *on your way to, before,* and *afterward.* Take a moment to breath fully *before* your important presentation; *while* you take the exam; *after* that tense phone call; and *as* you drive, listen and watch. You don't have to breathe deeply every breath. In fact, you won't breathe deeply when you mentally concentrate on something. Breathing shallowly helps hold the energy in your head, locks it into your muscles like when you lift weights. But you want to resume breathing fully when you stop concentrating. You can turn the transitions in your day into *reset moments*.

Think of all the transitions you have in a typical day: waking up, starting work, stopping to eat, getting out of the car, going to bed. Your day is filled with tasks and you can train yourself to breathe in the moments between them. Take a full belly breath *before* you take your first bite of breakfast; *after* you tie your shoes; and *as* you're getting kids off to school, changing classes, or milking a cow. Breathe as you park and get out of the car; breathe as you get into the car; breathe when you're stopped at stop lights. Arriving at your desk, meeting with someone, doing the dishes, climbing into bed—whatever your day has in it, it also has many transitions. Instead of making one phone call after another with no break, breathe after each call. Hang up and take a full breath before you dial the next number. Your voice will relax, you will think more clearly, and you will remember everything you need to say.

Every time you remember to breathe fully you create a reset moment. You pull energy out of your head, recirculate that energy throughout your body, and arrive in the present moment. Try it. It's free. I know from my own experience and the experience of everyone I know who has tried it that it shifts the way your life feels, for the better.

The challenge is to remember to practice breathing enough to reprogram your shallow-breathing habit. You can take a full, deep breath before you jump into an argument and after you've finished one. It's like a steam release valve or like pushing a reset button. When I get into my car and I have my hand on the door handle, I take a deep breath. This is my reset moment when I tell myself, "You're driving now, Denise. Be present." If all my energy is locked inside my head, my mind will grind away on its business and I won't be paying attention to the here and now, or to my driving. My body knows how to drive. I just need to give it energy to do it well.

The point is to recirculate the energy—i.e. bring it from the head back into the body by breathing deeply and fully from time to time. If you do this you will keep your energy flowing and wind up feeling much more vibrant and clear-headed at the end of the day. Try it. You'll see.

You can also choose to breathe when you have any "down" or "spare" or waiting time. I used to get frustrated and angry when I was kept waiting long for a doctor or dental appointment. I would think of all the things I could be doing instead and feel ill-used and disregarded. My breathing would get shallower and my blood pressure would rise. Now I don't *wait*. I use the time to breathe. Instead of getting more uptight the longer I wait, I get more relaxed as I breathe more. I do this if I get stuck in traffic, at the airport, and any time I would be "waiting." Learning to breathe turned a recurring "problem" into an opportunity—a gift of healing. If you stick with it, you will begin to notice a shift. It's subtle at first but the more you do it, the more you will notice your breathing expand and your sense of well-being enlarge.

An even simpler way to start expanding your breathing is with ten slow deep breaths as you're lying in bed trying to fall asleep. Simply release your belly and let your lungs fill from the bottom up, slowly and gently. Filling your lungs takes time. Your mind may resist at first but by the fourth or fifth slow, full breath, you may start to think, "Okay, that stuff I was fussing about can wait 'til tomorrow. Ahhhh!" Then Zzzzzzzzz.

☯

Now I'd like to show you the way I teach a person how listen to her body. Let's say I have Sam lying face down on my massage table. (Even though I'm talking about 'Sam', I'd like you picture yourself in this scene as much as you can.) When I first place my hands on her body, I gauge her general comfort/tension level by her breathing. I look to see how deeply the breath comes in. Her hips don't rise and fall with the breath so I ask her to breathe as deeply as she can. That helps some. I cannot force her to relax, and I need help from her breath to release the tension in her muscles. I see she is still breathing shallowly as only her chest moves as she breathes. There is more work we can do.

CHEST BREATHING

Maybe a more specific suggestion will help her shift her focus into her body and breathe deeply. I say, "You know how when you fill a bucket of sand, the sand goes to the bottom first and fills from the bottom up? Picture yourself filling up with air that same way, from your toes up." Her breath

BELLY BREATHING

deepens a bit more. Even if it takes the whole session to sink into that relaxed state where she's breathing deeply and slowly, it's worth it.

I want her to visualize what full breathing looks like. I ask: "Have you ever watched an infant breathe? It looks as if her whole body inhales and exhales. Her little belly expands and the little toes and hands quiver." She came into this world breathing fully with every part of her body, completely charged with life energy. As she grew and become socialized, she shut down her breathing and accumulated tension. She used to breathe fully and she can do it again. Remembering that ideal state can give her a model to work toward.

After she has begun to take a few deep breaths, I continue working. When I push on a tight area in her rump, I notice she has stopped breathing again. This is great for my demonstration. I say "There! You feel how tight that is there?" She grunts her agreement. "What about your breath?" I ask.

"I guess I was holding it," she says.

"So, what do you do if you want the tension to ease up?"

"Breathe!" she says, exhaling.

I love this part. This is when she starts to make the connection between holding her breath and holding in tension. I go on to find other tight spots. Sometimes she remembers to breathe into them and they loosen. When she does not breathe into the tension on her own, I pause to bring her attention back to the area that's stuck. I can feel her excitement as she finds her own breath and feels how it works to release the tension.

Now I ask her to turn over so she's lying face up on the treatment table. She's breathing a bit deeper but still doesn't fully fill her lungs when she takes a conscious breath. It clearly feels strange to take full breath when she is used to breathing so minimally. It's not a new mechanism after all, just an underused one. If she feels resistance, it may be that she doesn't want to admit how much she's been missing, how much she's been depriving herself of the energy she needs to thrive.

I ask her if she used to do the, "Look Mom, I'm fat" move.

she laughs and nods.

"Can you do that now?" I ask.

I can see her belly moving but it isn't puffing out. She breathes into her chest, pulls in her belly and says, "Like that?"

"No. Look at this." I stand back from the table and show her an exaggerated version of "belly breath." I puff my belly out as far as it can go, making my belly look about seven months pregnant. As my abdominal muscles expand, the diaphragm pulls down and brings air deep into my lungs. As I exhale, my belly flattens and my diaphragm pushes up on the lungs to push the air out—like a bellows. "You see, I flatten my belly from the bottom up, like emptying a toothpaste tube. The air doesn't actually go in and out of my belly; it just looks that way. See? My chest hardly moves at all."

She is feeling the sensations as she plays with this new idea. If she still has trouble, I might put her hand on my belly as I take an exaggerated belly breath so she can feel how much and how easily my belly moves. I might tell her the story about when I did my belly breath demonstration at a party.... I was showing several friends how I had finally learned to breathe deeply. I pulled my dress tighter around my middle and puffed out my belly as I took the deepest breath I could. "I haven't suddenly gotten fat," I explained. "It may look that way but it's just my diaphragm pushing my guts out of the way so the lower part of my lungs can expand with air." They laughed and tried to do the same thing. Twenty minutes later someone across the room started to smoke and a woman I didn't know shouted, "Wait! You can't light that, there's a pregnant woman in here!" We all looked around to find out whom she was talking about. She pointed at me and asked, "Aren't you almost due?" My friends and I burst out laughing as I explained that I wasn't pregnant—I was merely exaggerating the look of a full breath.

I understand Sam might not want to look fat, even temporarily, and I'm not advocating that she breathe like that all the time. The exaggerated belly pooching is only for when she is first re-opening her breathing. It's a jump-start action to reactivate the abdominal muscles. Once her body gets used to it, she can release her abdominal muscles and let her lungs fill downward without doing anything dramatic with her belly. And there's a good chance that as she uses those muscles more consistently to breathe, they will get firmer and her belly will become flatter. Mine did.

As Sam starts to breathe fully, she is startled by how much better it feels. The challenge now is to incorporate that new realization into daily life and make it a habit to breathe more. She has to breathe constantly to live and it simply takes attention and practice to reclaim her habit of *full* breathing. It's easy to revert to shallow breathing when the going gets tough but that can shift. I tell her, "If you remember nothing else here, remember this: **When in doubt, stick your belly out.**" If she keeps paying attention to her breath, the effects will amaze her.

If you do it, you will be amazed, too.

When your breathing expands, you stand straighter, your head lifts, and your posture and skin tone improve. Oxygen, energy and physical fluids can flow more freely within the tissues. The net effect is to open space in the body. With a little practice, breathing deeply comes easier. The more air you can easily pull into your lungs with each breath, over time the healthier you will become. It is a delight to see and feel the transformation take place.

Keeping this going doesn't have to take any time out of your daily schedule. You can deepen your breathing as you wait for an appointment, drive in the car, as you stand in an elevator, during television commercials, even during business meetings. Any break in the action can become an opportunity to focus inward and breathe. Imagine a bottleneck of people stuck in traffic all using the time to breathe deeply and relax rather then getting more tense and impatient. Deeper breathing could revolutionize the world! And it starts one breath at a time.

Now, before you go on to the next chapter, breathe. It doesn't matter that you just did it. As long as you're alive, you have to breathe—it's in your best interest to do it well. Wherever and however you are sitting as you read this, sit up a little straighter, throw out your belly, and take a deep breath. Smile. Hold that pose for a minute, breathing deeply. Try it now. You'll feel better.

Remember: When in doubt, stick your belly out!

CHAPTER 2—

Your Fabulous Body Electric

The Church says: The body is a sin.
Science says: The body is a machine.
Advertising says: The body is a business.
The Body says: I am a fiesta.

~ Eduardo Galeano

Your body *is* a fiesta. It has given you every experience of color, music, taste, texture, fragrance, and every sensual pleasure you've ever had. It's a whole universe of intelligent energy. It is your best ally for healing, and your best source of diagnostic information. You get fabulous results if you treat it as such. If you perceive your body as doing less than its best, you are mistaken about its very nature. It will heal you to the best of its ability until the moment of your death.

Spend a moment marveling at how your finger automatically heals from a cut. Think about how new life forms and grows in a woman's body without her giving it any instructions. Then there's the guy who breaks his back and relearns to walk despite what the doctors predicted. Your body is much more than a coordinated set of physical mechanisms. It is magical—and it has a much better handle on healing than your mind does.

Medical science measures healing energy in increased flow of blood, oxygen and endorphins. Some would call it "God's love" or chi. You experience it physically as warmth, full breath, a greater feeling of internal space, peace of mind, or relaxation. But that's just the tip of the iceberg. Once you understand and feel how healing energy flows in your body, you can learn to work with your own healing force and guide it to make your own miracles.

When I was a kid learning science, I was taught about *three* forms of matter: solid, liquid, and gaseous. These days, kids are taught about *four* forms of matter: solid, liquid, gaseous, and *electric*. Even the medical world is coming to see that the most important component of health is electric, in other words, the *flow of energy* through the body.

Our thoughts, emotions, and the invisible connections between every aspect of our being affect our health at the most fundamental level. They in turn affect the choices we make about what we eat, how we exercise, how we respond to "germs"—and everything else. The unconscious choices we make about how we think and feel, and how we breathe, dramatically affect whether that flow of energy increases or diminishes, and by how much. We know that viruses, polluted air, junk food, physical abuse, and poor body mechanics can wreck our health. Every bit as insidious is emotional abuse, everyday stress, and worry. Stress gums up the works—shuts down the flow of breath and energy. We need positive thoughts and love; exercise and rest; along with fresh air, clean water, clean food, and shelter to stay optimally healthy.

Your body is constantly communicating with you about your physical condition, giving you pleasure, and getting your attention with aches, pains and various symptoms. Some symptoms—like muscle soreness after your first time mountain climbing—are easy to understand and remedy. Other symptoms—such as increased difficulty with sleeping, a skin rash that appears "out of nowhere," or intermittent digestive upset—can be trickier to diagnose. Why? Because we are complex beings operating on several levels at once, and unresolved emotion may be part of the problem.

What about those emotional wounds we supposedly carry around? Perhaps we were not touched enough as we grew up or were not touched with respect and love. We might have grown up in the era when parents were told not to pick up their children when they cried for fear of spoiling them. Many have been beaten, molested, or had their physical boundaries violated in some horrific way. Such painful experiences teach us to stuff down unpleasant emotions and ignore the body because *feeling* hurts too much. We put up internal walls and carry on to survive the best way we knew how.

Then there's the nebulous wound that comes from not being seen for who we really are. Everyone has this to some extent. It's part of the human condition. So many childhood experiences serve to show us who we are not, thus teaching by contrast. It seems to be the work of adulthood to find out and come to terms with who we really are, then live from our authentic selves.

☯

If you have ever experienced "unexplained" back pain, or fibromyalgia[4], or chronic fatigue syndrome, or another set of symptoms that doctors could not easily diagnose, from my point of view, you are in luck. Not because these are pleasant things to go through but because your body and spirit are working so hard to teach you certain lessons. Complex and multi-level illnesses force you on a healing journey. If you persevere to learn those lessons, you are likely to reap huge rewards of insight and personal growth.

I want you to consider shifting your perspective on physical pain from seeing it as a problem to be avoided at all costs to seeing it as a sign of imbalance. From this point of view, pain is simply one of the louder ways your body communicates with you. Your body tells you in many quiet ways what you need for optimum health at every moment. The question is how much you listen to your body and give it what it says it needs. It is less painful to follow your body's advice *before* you hurt too much, but if you don't, your body will raise the "volume" of the pain until you *have to* pay attention.

Stiffness, small aches, and pains in your body are like rattling noises coming from your car. You can recognize something's loose and get it repaired immediately or you can put off the repairs until the car breaks down on the highway. As with your car, so it is with your body—it's your choice. From the outside, it seems easier and less expensive to pay attention to the warnings and take action in the early stages, but sometimes you resist

---

4   Fibromyalgia is a musculoskeletal disorder that causes pain, fatigue, and sleep disturbance. Medical science has not found a specific physical cause for it. Several intuitive massage colleagues and I agree that a common component among fibromyalgia patients is a marked need to be listened to.

doing what's in your best interest. Sometimes you choose to learn the hard way. Fortunately, the body is a brilliant teacher and, like many good teachers, it will shout at you (in the form of pain or disease) when all other attempts to get your attention fail.

Think of the many ways the body calls your attention to a problem. Nausea signals that the body can't process what's in the stomach. Vomiting indicates that the body has passed the overload point. Swelling and soreness indicate damage—say from a sprain or an infection—and that at least that specific area (if not the whole body) needs additional care and support as it works to repair the damage. Seen without a mental judgement such as "bad," "inconvenient," or "undesirable," symptoms appear to be just what they are: indications of imbalance and a call to repair.

I know a former waiter whose shoulder had been hurting for years from carrying heavy trays. He talked as if he resented his job. The pain was his body's way of telling him, "You aren't enjoying this. Find another job." He wanted to change jobs but didn't see an alternative. He used his shoulder just as strenuously to surf but his shoulder didn't hurt him then. He got massages to ease the tension in his muscles and keep him waiting tables but it was a temporary fix. His shoulder got so "bad" it even hurt him when he surfed and that's what made him finally look for different work. He changed jobs and is now happily doing strenuous physical work that he enjoys (as a massage therapist)—without shoulder pain. His body was always on his side, helping him make the changes his mind was too afraid to risk.

Our natural internal communication can become distorted by "normal" childhood experiences. Think about the messages many of us got about food as we grew up. We may not have

MASSAGE BY THE RIVER
"DEEP TISSUE IS OUR SPECIALTY"

HOW DEEP MIGHT YOU HAVE TO GO?

liked the way something smelled or felt in our mouth. Our body said, "No, don't eat that." But it was a vegetable, or Mom worked hard to prepare it, so we were forced, or at least coerced, to eat it. Maybe it was all we had. Maybe we knew we wouldn't be allowed to eat dessert without eating the meat, so we stuffed the meat in anyway, and then piled the dessert on top of that. Overload. In time, this overloading became a habit. We hear thousands of tempting advertisements that tell us to eat all the things they are selling. It's easy to form the habit of ignoring the small internal voice that tells us what we need to eat and instead buy into what advertisers tell us to eat. In other words, we stop listening to the guidance that would keep us healthy.

Now imagine a man, absorbed in a project at the office, working intently and constantly toward some deadline. He gets tired and sleepy earlier and earlier each night. His energetic batteries are running low. He has a harder time getting out of bed each morning; he is less mentally sharp during the day. His body is telling him, "I need rest." There's also a little voice inside saying, "Slow down and have some fun." But he no longer listens to that internal voice. In fact, he pushes all of his internal messages away for as long as he can get away with it. One morning he wakes up with back pain "out of nowhere" or "comes down with" a cold and wonders where that came from. This is his body insisting on what it needs, in its own terms. None of this is horrible or irreversible; in fact, it's *normal*. Once he clearly sees his patterns and choices, he can decide whether they still serve him or not.

I'm sure you can think of people who push themselves their whole lives, people who never stop to take care of themselves but are always driving toward some goal or taking care of everyone else. This pattern often comes from a childhood in which there was no choice but to push through adversity and meet the demands of others in order to survive. Or maybe an internal voice continually says, "You're not good enough. You have to do better." The point, though, is that as adults, we can choose differently. The patterns that served for survival in childhood are often self-destructive in adulthood. And the physical "problems" that come up are really the body's call to pay attention and heal. A mild heart attack, for example, can serve as a wonderful wake-up call, motivating a person to make healthy lifestyle changes and to move "Care for Self" higher on the priority list.

Fortunately, your body is standing by, capable of and ready to heal itself. Just as water will flow downhill even around obstacles if given the opportunity, your body will work to find a way to heal despite any abuse and neglect it has experienced. This is the magic, the spiritual imperative. Your body will tell you what it needs you to do—such as rest, drink more water, release pent-up emotions—to help restore the flow of energy and heal. Your job is to pay attention *inside* and do what it tells you to do.

So many of us are wandering around with parts of ourselves defended and shut-down. And still—lovingly, persistently—the inner voice is working to show us how to heal—often in the form of dreams. The following story gives a glimpse at what it looks like when your body starts to call.

A Briefcase Full of Blues

One day a dark, hairy man, 5′ 8,″ 210 lbs, flumped down on my table, clearly dissatisfied about something. He didn't make eye-contact with me, his head hung down, and his shoulders sagged. His external body language said, "I'm depressed." I figured he was in his mid-fifties and, by the sound of his vowels, from New York. He told me he was an attorney. As I began working, I opened my receptivity and waited for his story to unfold.

He was a person with massive tension. He had dense muscles sheathed in fat and packed with emotional energy. His shoulders were screaming with stuck energy, and he was breathing shallowly. His mind had a stranglehold on his energy and wasn't letting him relax. He came to me for relief so I looked for an opening.

"When did you arrive on Maui?"

"Six days ago."

"Wow, you're still this tight after six days of vacation! Good thing you came for bodywork. See if your breath can go a little deeper. Imagine pulling in the air and energy all the way down to your toes." I breathed with him. Once his breath had deepened somewhat I asked, "How do you feel about being an attorney?"

"My father is an attorney."

"So?"

"I passed the BAR last year. Now I'm working in my father's firm." I felt energy surge through his back. "I never had a choice!"

"Your father sounds like a pretty powerful guy." *I was sure I didn't know the half of it.* "How old are you?"

"Twenty-eight, last month."

"Twenty-eight! Your body feels more like your father's age." He made a little snort of assent. "He's a little grayer."

"So you've become your father?"

"That's his plan."

"But that's not what you want. You don't want to practice law?"

"I never had a choice," he repeated sullenly.

"What do you want to do with your life?"

"I keep having this dream. I'm alone, walking up and down the beach, with a metal detector, just sifting through the sand. That's all I want to do."

"Just walk along the beach with a metal detector?"

"That's it."

"Well, at least that's clear. You want to search, on your own."

When he turned over, I was stunned to see the face of a young man. He had beautiful hazel eyes under those copious dark brows. He really was 28. "Aaron, you need to start taking care of yourself. You're a young man! What do you do for exercise?"

"I play a little racketball." Now he was watching me intently.

I said, "You've proven you can do it, be a lawyer. Now you have plenty of time to do whatever you want with the rest of your life."

"I never wanted to be a lawyer, that's for sure."

"Do you know what you might want to do instead?"

"Just walk with a metal detector." He laughed.

"Okay, well, give yourself permission. You need to start finding your own answers. The world's a big place. You have options. I can feel in your body all the misery and resentment you've been stuffing down for so long. You can start letting that stuff go. Breathe deeply. Drink lots of water and get more bodywork. You'll feel a whole lot better."

When he got up off the table, I suggested he go for a walk on the beach. He took my hand warmly and shook it. I gave him a hug. His dreams were prompting him to search for his own answers. I got to serve as another signpost, encouraging him to follow his own path. I thought of Richard Bach's words:

> You stand outside the circle and wonder why you feel left out, unaware that you need your own permission to join the others, not theirs. And sometimes there are those who love themselves enough to pull you into the circle."[5]

I was pulling Aaron back into the circle.

---

5   From Illusions by Richard Bach; (Dell, New York, 1977).

EXERCISE 2: **Marvel at Your Miracle**

1. Think of three things that amaze you about your body.

Women, if you've given birth, perhaps the most obvious one is that you can make another human inside your body. Marvel at what a miracle it is that your body knew what to do without any mental intervention on your part. Men, marvel that each drop of your semen has the potential to create thousands of lives. If your body is not able to reproduce itself physically and you have an issue with that, please take this opportunity to marvel at all the things your body *can* do. If you can drive a car, marvel at that. It takes a ferociously complicated set of operations to drive at all. And somehow most of us manage to do it. You have to step on the accelerator just the right amount to control the car's rate of speed; step on a brake pedal just the right amount, at the right time; turn the steering wheel just the right amount, at the right time; shift the gears if it's a standard transmission; see the other cars (and pedestrians) plus calculate their rates of speed and direction; make adjustments with your feet on the pedals; move your hands on the wheel; maybe flick the turn signal; look in your rear-view mirror to see yet more cars and make adjustments in all those things according to the new information constantly coming in. It's a marvel of mental and physical coordination. You were right as a teenager to be proud of yourself for learning to drive. Safely driving through traffic is an amazing feat.

Now, take five minutes and start a list of the amazing things you can do with your body. Imagine being without the use of any parts of your body—legs, eyes, kidneys— and realize what a blessing it is that you have them. I have a friend who regularly crawls on the floor, pretending she has no legs, any time she feels badly about her body. That exercise puts all the things she can do into perspective for her.

2.   Think of the marvel of juggling, of chopping an onion—even brushing your teeth. These tasks require a stunning coordination of hands, eyes and timing. A friend of mine makes 30-foot aerial jumps with his kiteboard. I find this a fantastic thing for a body-mind to do. We are able to do so many amazing things with our bodies that we take for granted. Take a few minutes and think of all the things you couldn't do without your wonderful body.

3.   Now think of three things that your body does that give you exquisite pleasure. It could be smelling a hot pumpkin pie; tasting a juicy summer peach; feeling the smooth suppleness of a baby's skin. There's the obvious one of orgasm. I love the feeling of my hair blowing back when I'm running fast. What about drinking a glass of cool water when you're hot and thirsty? We could drink water without also feeling pleasure—but we feel pleasure as a bonus. I thank my body daily for all the wonderful things I can do with it. See how many times today you can marvel at the pleasure your body gives you. Then thank it.

4. Cultivate the habit of appreciating your body for all the things it can do and all the pleasures it gives you. Every day, thank it for all it has done for you. This simple practice will have a profound effect on your overall well-being.

Now throw your belly out, breathe, and smile.

☯

CHAPTER 3—

The Gift of Breakdown

Soul enters life from below, through the cracks finding an opening into life at the points where smooth functioning breaks down.

~ Thomas Moore

Think of the epic stories you've heard. An epic journey begins with a problem, a tear in the normal fabric of life. Maybe the hero wants to avenge the death of his father, maybe a monster has snatched his beloved, or maybe he feels a yearning to go on a holy quest. The hero may not even know his final goal, but something in his life has reached the breaking point and he has to set out. He (or she) doesn't know exactly what he's up against but realizes there will be danger and difficulty along the way. The heroic part is that he knows the journey is going to be tough but he sets out anyway and keeps going, facing fear and the unknown, until his goal is met.

Without an obstacle, without hardship or something breaking down, there would be no need for a journey. When everything's calm and copacetic, we sit around and grow fat. Adversity is a marvelous motivator. When the princess gets kidnapped, the prince has to go rescue her; he grows and learns valuable lessons along the way. Similarly, a life-threatening illness such as cancer can serve as a great motivator to clean up one's diet, habits, and relationships, and rearrange major priorities.

The great epic stories are also metaphors for the personal journey we go on when we decide to meet our internal monsters and shine light on our personal demons. Each of us has a dark side—Carl Jung called it our Shadow—traits and feelings that we'd rather not own up to. This is the stuff society says we are not *"supposed"* to feel—everything from not wanting to share with a sibling, to hating an overbearing or needy mother, to a desire to hurt our own child. Being violated feels bad enough, but what if part of the experience felt good somehow? What if we enjoyed watching someone we care about get hurt? Sometimes we yearn to take good care of ourselves but do self-destructive things instead and then feel guilty or inadequate. Those conflicting emotions shut us down even more, both physically and emotionally. These are the very monsters we must face, the stuck energy we have to move through, in order to get to the light and the freedom beyond them.

The easiest way to approach scary inner wounds is by gaining confidence with smaller ones first. The "issues" that have many layers of different emotion and have perhaps been compounded by repetition over time, usually carry a lot of energy and can be deeply challenging. You don't have to tackle these first. Begin with something easier, something less "hot." For example, you might look at why you are stingy in certain situations or why you feel the need to show off around certain people. The first step is to notice your feelings when they come up.

You've probably been to a party or gathering and bumped

YOU NEED A VACATION LARRY. HERE ARE TWO TICKETS TO CABO, ONE FOR YOU, AND ONE FOR YOUR STRESS HUMP.

into someone you usually try to avoid. The next time this happens you can turn this small event into an exercise that can help you—and have fun doing it. Decide that this time you'll tune inward and pay attention. This time, instead of ducking out, greet the person and notice how you feel. Do your shoulders tighten? Does your breathing get shallower? Perhaps the woman says something that makes you feel defensive. You remind yourself to breathe. The defensive feeling passes through you without any further reaction. You feel more space in your body and notice she seems tense and uncomfortable herself. You sincerely tell her you like her earrings. She smiles, disarmed. You feel stronger being generous and you excuse yourself to get some water. You decide you don't have to avoid her next time. Instead of feeling diminished, you feel bigger. It was a small encounter and a success. Maybe the next time you see her, she comes over to you to say something nice and you accept it. You may or may not become friends but the negative charge is gone. You can feel the internal smile. You've reversed the negative pattern.

As you gain practice noticing your discomfort in the moment and allowing yourself to feel it, you stop amplifying the discomfort. In fact, this approach teaches you to soften your resistance to "negative" feelings and it takes the sting out of them. With this kind of practice, you can build the strength and skill to tackle even your darkest demons. The key is practice.

One of my own personal demons has been impatience. It may not be one of the seven deadly sins, but it has given me all manner of trouble. I've been impatient with others and impatient with myself. My healing process was always too slow for my liking. I'm willing to brave hardship, fight monsters, and jump through hoops of fire—but I want to do it and get it over with. I want to be healed already. My healing journey is teaching me patience, because that's the lesson I need to learn. And I'm stubborn enough that it takes breakdown to get me to stop my forward momentum and pay attention to what needs healing. The delicious irony is that as I am becoming more patient with myself and with life's processes, I resist the process less and I am healing faster.

The valuable lessons are often the hardest won. This is partly because you get out of a situation what you put into it and partly because human lessons involve overcoming resistance, often in the form of fear. If you are afraid of making mistakes and public exposure, getting up in front of a crowd and giving a speech is a heroic undertaking. If you love attention and adrenaline-pumping thrills, quieting yourself to sit in meditation with nothing to look at but your innermost self requires huge courage. It is in recognizing your fear and facing it anyway that it dissolves. Your resistance is an indication of how dear the lesson is to you and perhaps how much breakdown might have to happen before you are willing to make the changes you know you need to make. The less you resist, the less you create drama and breakdown, and the easier it is to learn the lesson.

Anything pushed beyond its limit will eventually break down. If you look at those times your own body has broken down, you'll probably see that you got signals ahead of time about what you needed. Your body warned and guided you, but you did not heed the warnings and respond appropriately. Breaking down in the middle of a busy life is usually a sign that you have effectively turned off the guidance system that keeps your mind and body working together in functional balance.

In this fast-paced culture, it's easy to lose touch with yourself. We high-tech humans don't always feed ourselves when we're hungry, even though we can. We don't always sleep when we need rest. If we are under the pressure of a work deadline, we may put off sleep for hours, even days. Our minds and wills get very skilled at overriding our physical impulses and ignoring the ways our bodies tell us about our physical needs. We unconsciously disconnect internally because doing so helps us get the job done. This artificial rearranging of priorities keeps us disconnected from our inner guidance system.

Imagine a toddler who is hungry and tired, trying to get the attention of his busy mom, who is talking on the phone. His movements start to become uncoordinated. Then he knocks something over in frustration. It's hard for him to run on empty. If the mother were paying attention to his body language, she would recognize that he is nearing breakdown. She notices his frustration, but the phone call is important enough to her that she puts him off. He makes more noise and then picks up the phone; he bumps her leg and tugs on her clothes. He gets increasingly louder and more annoying until the mother can't tune him out any longer. She yells at him to stop pestering her. He retreats for a few moments but he needs her help to get his needs met and can stand them going unmet for only so long. He's approaching a tantrum and getting him back to equilibrium will become increasingly difficult. The body's path to breakdown is essentially the same as a child's. If as an adult you continually put your mental agenda before your physical and emotional agenda, your body will escalate the severity of your physical symptoms until you *have* to pay attention. It's so much easier on yourself if you listen to your body before you get to that point.

I've worked on several surgeons whose muscles feel as though they're chronically dehydrated and who can't take a full breath when asked. In medical school, where there's so much competition and pressure to do the super-human, doctors often learn to work when they're exhausted and put their own bodies' needs at the bottom of the priority list rather than becoming role models for excellent self-care.

Part of learning to function in a complex society includes learning to subordinate personal needs sometimes, but there needs to be balance. Taking great physical and emotional care of yourself doesn't always have to be at the top of your to-do list but it doesn't belong at the bottom, either.

Healing is a practice sport. You will have moments of breakthrough and you'll probably have breakdown as well. Healing happens in layers, and often one layer of an issue must be healed before you have access to the next layer. If you aren't finding healing answers on one level, you must look on another. An epic journey involves challenges on many fronts and a healing epic is no different. If the strictly physical, medical model doesn't have an answer for you, or has only part of the answer, you have to keep looking, perhaps at alternative methods, perhaps in the spiritual or emotional realms. The breakthrough happens in the moment when you, the hero or heroine, are cornered and all your customary skills and resources no longer work—at the moment of impasse, or crisis, or breakdown. This is the moment there is nothing to do but surrender and ask for help. Your personality ego just doesn't have all the answers. This is when you call on a higher power, *the deeper power within your self.*

Your own intuition is your conduit to that power and a fantastic ally in your quest for wholeness. It's your gut feeling, your most immediate tool to zero in on what's going on in your body and the healing action you need to take. [See Chapter 8 for a more thorough discussion of intuition.] If you need more help, you can enlist a healer's intuition. The best medical doctors I know use their intuition to guide them in applying their knowledge and experience. You may not be ready for what a given healer has to offer at a given moment, or you may go to a healer who doesn't have access to the level where you need healing. That's okay. That simply means you need to keep searching. The way I see it, if you are alive, your healing journey is not over.

Breakdown can happen at the moment of wounding or it can take years to surface. When you are young and vulnerable, if a trauma overwhelms you, you build defenses and strategies to work around the unresolved wound and carry it until there's an opportunity to address it. Eventually the wound resurfaces in some form to be healed.

Now I'll tell you the story of my own deep wound, how and why *my* internal communicative link got severed. In a way I'm lucky. The break happened at such a young age and it was so dramatic, it compelled me to begin my healing journey relatively early in life. I think of it as my own "big bang."

I Will Breathe No More

In this story about intuitive healing, I am the client. Among other things, it shows that the insights from a healing session can come long after the session itself. The session creates the opening and the healing energy continues to shift things—sometimes for quite a while.

I'd been piecing together the story of my birth my whole life. I was given up for adoption at birth. My birth-mother was unconscious for the birth and neither touched nor saw me after I was born; then I was immediately whisked away to wait for my family in foster care. As an adult, I traveled across the U.S. to meet the doctor who delivered me, corresponded with social workers who handled my case, and eventually found and got to know my birth mother. She gave me information about her pregnancy and her family but my experience and what it meant to me was mine to explore.

I had breathing problems including severe allergies and asthma since I was little. I had been working to heal them since my teenage years. In my thirties, while doing a healing exercise, I had had a vision of myself as an infant lying in a crib and peering out through the bars. I was breathing as little as I could, not feeling any emotion. Later, I realized this might have been the moment I shut down my breathing in order not to feel the pain of abandonment or the fear that no one would ever come love me.

In the moment of that vision (perhaps a few weeks after birth), I lay in a crib, having not bonded with anyone, afraid, and longing for love. The disappointment, pain and outrage of abandonment had probably become so intense that I limited my breathing in order to stop feeling the emotions that hurt so much. I was placed with my adoptive family when I was six weeks old, but by then the pattern seems to have been set. As a child, I was not very emotional; I was "smart" and lived in my head.

Ever since I had the insight that linked my breathing and allergic problems with my birth trauma, I had been looking for ways to get to clear the issue and feel better. Understanding the possible cause was an important first step but the mental connection alone didn't shift what was going on in my body. I had high hopes for a Transformational Breathwork session with my friend Meg, who was familiar with both my personal history and my determination to heal. Meg has a PhD in polymer physics plus a driving interest in alternative healing, and the healing technique she knew is specifically designed to unlock emotional trauma using the breath—where I knew I was stuck. Our intention was to release the energetic knot that was causing my allergic symptoms if we could.

First, we cleared the middle of the room and set up a futon to work on. Meg had me do some exercises to increase my respiration: I raised my arms, bent down to the floor and deliberately breathed fast and hard. Nothing much happened. We tried more exercises. I could tell by Meg's frustration that I wasn't getting as worked up as she wanted me to. (I told her that I didn't let myself *get* worked up, that was part of the problem.) Finally I lay down on the futon and she put her hands under my back while she showed me how she wanted me to breathe—fast and shallow, almost to hyperventilation. I kept breathing as best I could.

Meg stroked my forehead. "Picture yourself in that crib," she directed. "Keep breathing. What do you feel?"

"Scared. Abandoned. Where's my mother? This isn't how it's supposed to be." I wasn't "thinking." I was in that non-rational, non-judgmental state where impressions came and I just spoke them.

"Let's go back," Meg said. This was Meg's intuition guiding her. "It started earlier." I could tell she was tuned in. "Go back to when you were still in the womb. What's that like?"

"I feel hated. It's all my fault."

"Yes, somebody blames you. Can you tell who that is?"

"Aunt Betty, her aunt. It must be her." (My mother stayed with Aunt Betty through the pregnancy.) "She feels I'm the one who caused all the problems."

Meg snorted, "But you weren't even born yet!"

"My birth mother was so young and you know those times… Betty felt I caused my mother's fall from grace," a part of me explained. (I had met Betty once and knew her general disapproval of the situation but had never felt it viscerally). "I guess I got the full brunt of the aunt's frustration and hatred. God, it's so strong!" I started to curl up.

"Keep breathing," she prompted.

"She wants me dead. She wishes I would just die."

"How does your mother feel?"

"Sometimes she loves me, sometimes she hates me. She feels both. But Aunt Betty keeps saying I shouldn't be alive. It feels like I'm getting kicked." I could barely breathe.

"Literally? Keep breathing," she said.

"No, with her energy. I feel her hatred. I shouldn't be here." I wasn't crying. It was as if I understood the emotions but didn't *feel* them. "Am I blocking out my feelings?" I asked.

"No! Those are *her* feelings," Meg said. "Not even your mother's. You're supposed to be here." She stroked my hand.

"It's not just Aunt Betty, it's the whole family," I gasped. "They think I shouldn't exist, that I have no right to live."

"Breathe! Do you as that baby think you shouldn't be here?"

"No. I don't know. It feels so scary." My breath got shallower again. "All that hostility! And hatred."

"Come on, breathe with me. You're backing away from it." Meg again pushed me to breathe fast and deeply. I couldn't sustain it. Finally she said, "Your mother didn't nourish herself very well."

"No, I don't think she did. She was so ambivalent."

That was as far as we got in that session. I spent the next weeks sloshing around in those impressions of anger, fear, and ambivalence. I was fascinated by the idea of getting impressions from the womb, *my* experience in the womb. I didn't care that there's no way to *prove* the validity of what I had just experienced. It *felt* true. And it explained to me a lot about my way of dealing with abandonment and rejection. We had another session but it didn't reveal any new insights. I still had trouble getting to that hyped-up, open, emotional state through my breathing. I started to understand the pain I had felt and how it had motivated my life up to then. I eventually talked to my birth mother, who confirmed that she was ambivalent about how she felt about my life and her eating reflected that.

I began to see that all those hostile feelings directed toward me belonged to my extended biological family. I didn't have to claim them as my own. I certainly hadn't done anything to deserve them. I also didn't have to be angry about that feeling of unworthiness I'd always carried. Now that I saw where it all came from, I could bless and release it, send it back to Original Source. Not so much root it out as put it in its proper place; not overshadowing my life, but quietly on a shelf as part of my life's lessons.

Eventually I stopped seeing myself as unwanted, or that I shouldn't be here. That was Aunt Betty's lack of love, not mine—nor was it even my birthright. If my birth-mother bought into her aunt's perspective, that was her choice. These days I find that I am less angry in general and less apt to over-defend myself, specifically. I cycle back around into feelings of unworthiness but now have a peg to hang them on. I found that my sneezing and congestion were symptoms of emotional and respiratory shutdown and I work with my breath to open it back up. My allergic symptoms were reduced by about 70 percent in the months that followed. Since that time, I've done more breathing work that has cleared the allergies by about 95 percent and my breathing is continuing to expand as I clear out my deeper emotional holding patterns.

We all have experienced the pain of unlovingness from authority figures. But we don't have to carry that pain or stay stuck in that pattern of feeling unworthy. Here's an exercise to re-pattern messages of unworthiness and replace them with expanded love and compassion for yourself.

EXERCISE 3A: **Be Your Own Best Parent**

In your chair or wherever you are, read the next few paragraphs to understand the exercise. It would be best if you can have someone read these instructions to you slowly while you do the exercise. You can also do it on your own. Just make sure you set aside at least 30 minutes and familiarize yourself with the sequence beforehand so you don't have to interrupt it too often to look at the book. If you do it repeatedly, you can get really good at it and gain invaluable insights.

1. Clear some space for yourself and get comfortable. Maybe lie on a bed or sofa. Unbutton your pants, take off your shoes, and generally make sure nothing is restricting you or your breathing. If you need to, go to the bathroom or get a drink of water before you begin.

2. Feel inside. Close your eyes. Are your shoulders tight? Does your belly feel full? Scan your body to see what's going on NOW.

3. Breathe fully and deeply. Throw out your belly and gently pull in as much air as you can. Expand your lungs.

Imagine air and energy as water filling up all your inner spaces.

Imagine a time when you felt small or restricted or helpless. Imagine a time when you needed to be rescued or loved or simply *seen*.

4. Feel the intensity of those feelings. Breathe. Nod to the pain of it. Acknowledge to yourself that you didn't get what you needed and let that be the simple truth without blaming anyone.

5. Imagine you, as your grown up self, coming into the scene with your child self and giving your small, younger self what you needed then. If you needed someone to defend you, play the scene as if your big self steps in and saves the day. If you needed to be held and comforted, have your grown up self pick up the smaller you and hold and comfort yourself. In your imagination, give yourself what you didn't get originally. Get creative. Be generous with yourself. That wounded aspect of yourself may need lots of encouragement and love, over and over. Your mind may balk at this idea but sincerely try it once and you'll feel relief.

6. Remember to do this when you feel yourself shrinking inside, whenever you catch yourself reacting from a wound in your past. There are probably many layers of pain and different unloving messages to resolve. The more you do this, the more you will fill gaps in your early experiences with love. You will feel how truly magnificent you are. You will become increasingly alive inside!

I've gone back to that crib scene and rocked my infant self many, many times. My infant self has since gotten plenty of energetic kisses and hugs, and every time I feel better.

The human blueprint says we're born whole, with our minds and bodies in fully open communication. As infants, when we needed to poop, we pooped. We didn't have to raise our hands to get permission or think about it, we just did it. As we grew up and had to navigate the world, we developed our minds and we become socialized, necessarily. Over time, with the input of information, social mores, parental expectation, and peer pressure, our mind started to run the show. Even though mind and body still "talk" to each other, the physical voice becomes like background noise, and, as adults, we ignore it until the body cranks up the volume to get our attention with pain or other symptoms.

To illustrate what I mean about the mind and body having two voices, imagine you've been driving for an hour and a half on a busy highway, you're late for a wedding, and your body signals, *Gotta pee*. You mind responds, *Not here—hold it—tighten the muscles—keep going*. This "dialog" happens in an instant and is concise and graceful. You may not notice it because it has become unconscious but it's as if you have two drivers at the wheel, your physical *ego* and your mental *ego*, battling for which one will steer the whole system. The body will cooperate with the mind as long as it can, and then well, you gotta pee. With luck, by then you will have pulled off the highway. Your mind and body don't have to be at odds, however, it simply takes an adjustment of perspective to realign the two. In other words, you have to listen and reacquaint yourself with those submerged parts of yourself. They will give you valuable insights and help you become whole.

Our action-oriented society insists that we constantly produce, go forward, and give out. The media and our culture say that if we let go or let down or "drop the ball," we will lose whatever advantage we have already gained. We are taught to take but not to receive. Our habit of frenzy is so ingrained that simply stopping to receive nurturing or loving touch can feel strange or even scary. We need to balance driving forward and pressure with rest and gentleness.

What would it take to get you to slow down and look within? Do you need to break down first? Are you willing to unlock the door to your inner pain and inner joy *before* breakdown happens? You can do that if you create space for healing. Even amidst your busy life, you can create opportunities to set down your burdens. You can give yourself permission to rest and replenish your energy in gentle, nurturing ways. You *can* give yourself moments of respite to balance the busy-ness with calmness and reconnect with a feeling of wholeness. You simply have to decide that you will.

This means allowing blank spaces in your schedule and time that is not allocated to being productive. This means turning off the cell phone more often, leaving work early, taking time to go for a walk, getting a massage. Massage is a wonderful forum for learning to receive, go inside, and balance the mental-masculine *yang* with the emotional-feminine *yin* sides of yourself. Yoga is great, so is *tai chi*. These practices encourage you to be still, and to balance active and dynamic with passive, and receptive. They are so popular now because they offer the quiet, inner space we all desperately need.

It may seem obvious to you that your friend's lower back pain is a call for her to rest and take better care of herself, but when your own back hurts do you stop and look at ways to rest and balance your own life? You might realize that you overuse your right shoulder or that you habitually sit too long at the computer without getting up and stretching. But do you adjust your schedule to take care of yourself unless you're forced to by pain and dysfunction? One of life's challenges is to recognize and relearn your own inner language, and to follow your body's whisperings to improve your health. If your body didn't break down, you'd simply die one day when your body had reached the point of no repair and you'd miss learning valuable lessons.

If I resist something I need for too long—like rest—my body-mind will force the issue by breaking down. But I'd rather *prevent* breakdown by heeding my personal warning signs and being willing to make changes without the trauma. For example, if I'm overdoing it and feel like I'm approaching a "cold", it's so much more fun to take a day off to rest and recharge my batteries *before* my body shuts me down for three days with miserable symptoms.

With migraines, I found that once I let my stress level get past a certain point (dehydration was consistently a factor) and a migraine was looming, there was no way to will it away. My body was already *in tantrum*. I began to surrender to the migraine process and ride it out without resisting it. And then the breakthrough happened. When I accepted what was happening in the moment, I heard my body tell me to stop, and drink water. Now if I feel a migraine coming on, I stop what I'm doing, immediately drink a quart of water, lie down, and drink another quart soon. While I lie down, I breathe deeply and stay focused in my body. I headed off migraines that way for years until I stopped having them altogether. Gradually I learned how to take better care of myself, including breathing and resting when life gets hectic and especially staying hydrated, so I don't start the migraine cycle in the first place. Now that I mention it, now is a great time for a drink of water. How about a glass for you?

We've all had times of breakdown in some way or another. The following exercise is a way to practice owning your experience instead of feeling at the affect of. It is also a great way to spin the negative energy associated with that breakdown to a positive direction. It is an important part of healing.

EXERCISE 3B: Blessing Breakdown

1. Take a deep breath. Think back to a time when you physically broke down, when you pushed your body too hard or ignored its warning signs, and you paid dearly for it. Maybe you kept hiking on a twisted ankle and injured it to the point where you couldn't walk for weeks. Maybe you knew you needed a rest but kept working until a really bad flu brought you to your knees. Perhaps you've had cancer or a heart attack or an illness that forced you to make radical changes in the way you do things. Spend some time thinking about what lead up to the "problem" and then what happened as a result. Did you get some needed rest time? Revamp your diet? Get into better shape?

Take another breath.

2.   Think of symptoms you've experienced that were warning signs for more serious breakdown. Remember times you *did* heed their warning. Have you ever taken time off work to rest *before* your got really sick? Think of the ways you prevent physical breakdown. Give yourself credit for brushing your teeth regularly, drinking water throughout the day, and any time you forego junk food for a healthy snack.

3.   If you haven't already given thanks to your body for giving you physical limits and enforcing them, thank your body now.

4.   Now, think of an episode of *emotional* breakdown in your life. Start with a simple episode that had a beginning, a middle, and an end. Maybe you felt increasingly undervalued at work, got fed up, and left that job to find a much better one. Perhaps you went through a period of depression or felt like you simply couldn't take life anymore. If you couldn't understand what was going on at the time, do you understand now why it happened? Can you see it as a lesson learned, as a blessing? Trace the feelings that lead to the breakdown, through the breakdown itself, and how you felt afterward.

If you can't think of an example in your own life, look at a time a loved-one had an emotional breakdown of some sort and came out much better in the end. That can be easier to see. Even though upheaval and trauma are uncomfortable, they are often the catalyst for much-needed changes.

5. The point is to shift your perspective on breakdown to appreciation. The less you resist it, the sooner it can do its work and you will have the benefit from it. See if the next time you break down in some way, you can smile and see what benefit there might be in it. This shift is likely to surprise and delight you.

CHAPTER 4—

Listening To Your Body

After years, at any moment, our bodies
are ready to remember us.

~ Anne Michaels

If you notice that your body is not as healthy as you would like it to be, then you may need to look at its working conditions and listen to what it has to say. The connected, conscious listening that I'm talking about is an active process. Learning (or relearning) your body's language requires *paying attention* to your aches and pains, *listening* to what your body is telling you to do ,and then *doing* it—even if that simply means taking a deep breath. When you are lovingly connected to your body, there is no break in the action between getting the message and responding.

So, what form does this communication take? Your body constantly sends out signals, which describe your energy levels, emotional states, internal chemistry, and what you need to balance them. Upright posture, radiant skin, and vibrant energy are clear, external signs of good health. You can see that a person is tired by her droopy eyelids, sagging shoulders, and circles under the eyes—in other words, by her external "body language." Your body also constantly sends information about your own health to you *internally*. You feel tiredness in your own body as a dullness, and in your thoughts as an overall slowness or heaviness. Muscle soreness after work or exercise tells you that you pushed past your limit. A tight or uneasy feeling in your belly warns you not to do what you're considering.

Your body constantly gives you signals about how you feel but you ignore most of them when you're busy focusing on whatever is going on in front of you, when you're "in your head." You know the more obvious signals, such as your tummy rumbling to signal you need to eat. Your rump goes numb or your back gets stiff to signal that you've been sitting too long and need to move around. Your eyes get dry and itchy to let you know you've done enough reading or staring at a screen. The question is, *Do you pay attention to these signals and do something to help your body when it tells you to?* What changes would you have to make to answer, "yes" to that question?

Throughout your childhood, adults tell you *not* to do what your body tells you *to* do, like wiggle, poke, and shout. As you grow, your body seems to betray you by farting at embarrassing times, getting pimples, growing too fast. Then there are the kids on the playground, TV, magazines, and the Internet that make sure you know everything that's "wrong" with your body. "Your penis isn't big enough so take our pills to enlarge it." "Your skin isn't smooth enough so buy this cream to tighten it." "You're too fat, buy these diet pills." ...

You know what I'm talking about.

From childhood on, if someone beats you or dis- respects your body, you tend to judge it as ugly, imperfect, unworthy— even evil. This can get heavy as negative thoughts

CONSCIOUS THOUGHT

EMOTIONS

EMOTIONS

PHYSICAL RESPONSE

The flow of energy

and judgments pile up. With all that, it's no surprise if as an adult you have a hard time listening to and trusting your body's impulses. In modern society, it is "normal" to neglect your body, sometimes to the point of self-abuse. But it doesn't have to be that way. Your body *is* a fiesta! Even if it's two hundred pounds overweight, even if it has tremors, even if it is missing limbs, it is a wonder. It does so many things beau- tifully and you are lucky to have it. Your body is constantly giving you information about its working conditions, its state of health, and your emotions. Your "gut" reactions to people and situations around you are often the most reliable informa- tion you can get. Wherever you are in your relationship with your body, you can work with it and become its partner by simply listening to its signals.

The first step is to notice how you aren't listening to your body. Look for large and small ways you are self-destructive with yourself. It's only when you identify those that you can start to shift them. Then recognize the ways you are good to your body. Create more of those, and enjoy them.

☯

This exercise is the beginning of an important shift toward being in your body and listening to your emotions. At first you will have to mentally pay attention, again and again. The goal is to get comfortable with listening inside.

EXERCISE 4: Listening to Your Body

1. Today, sometime in the next twenty-four hours, notice yourself feeling uncomfortable about something, something small that you would normally brush aside. Maybe your back feels tight as you head home from work. You don't have to *do* anything about it, just notice it. Maybe you told yourself you would limit yourself to one cappuccino today and you notice a twinge of guilt as you order your third one. Perhaps a guy in the elevator leers at you and you want to tell him off, but you look down instead. Rather than rush into your head back to the next thought, pause for a moment and really feel the anger, or vulnerability or injustice in your body. Sometimes the frustration is directed at yourself for not listening to and acting on your gut feelings.

2. Congratulate yourself that you have the courage to feel your feelings. Every time you do feel inside, appreciate that you made the effort and it's working. It's tricky to notice these things and stay with them because the thoughts and emotions pass through quickly and you want to bury any discomfort as soon as possible. Your mind wants to race forward to the next thing. But you can do it. You can feel those feelings. They won't kill you.

MEGAN'S BODY TAKES DESPERATE MEASURES

3.   For the next three days, see if you can catch your body giving you signals that tell you when you've overstepped a healthy boundary with yourself. Every time you do, see it as a positive step toward reclaiming the vitality and presence you were born with. Whatever pain or injustice or irritation you felt pales in comparison to the victory of reclaiming your ability to feel in the moment. Now take a deep breath.

4.   **Advanced level:** See if you can trace the discomfort you notice back to its origin. Even if you can only go one layer deeper, that's a start. In the cappuccino example above, the discomfort came from not honoring a decision to take better care of yourself. Think of examples in your life where you have not honored your well-being, or have done some self-sabotage. If you can think of several examples, recognize there's pattern there. Okay. So it is. Don't judge it. Just let it be. After you accept it, you can change it if you choose to.

5. Now see if you can remember a time you did something really nurturing for yourself and compare the feelings. There's probably a pattern there, too. And you have a choice between the two. Recognize that you sometimes make self-destructive choices, and rather than beat yourself up about it, simply choose to be good to yourself as much as possible, from now on. Better yet, get up and do something nurturing for yourself right now. Drink a glass of water, take a hot bath—at least take a few deep breaths. Yes, breathe right now! Smile at yourself. You're expanding.

6. In the elevator example, there may be many layers of disempowering experiences. Allow yourself to consider ways your life has taught you that you don't have personal power. You may have been punished when you exerted independence or belittled when you did something well. Whatever your history, ask yourself if that's what you choose now. Keep listening for feelings of disempowerment and honor them. You have probably been in truly disempowering situations. They serve to teach by contrast. Look for feelings of success and power and ways to reinforce your choice of wellness.

7. Whatever is going on externally, let the feeling in your body guide you to what's really going on *inside you*. In the next few days, see if you can notice when your body gives you subtle signals of discomfort telling you to pay attention to something and signals of joy when you do. The point is not to *do* anything different but to notice what it feels like *inside* and not retreat from it. Action can come after, if you want. I bet you'll be impressed at what you learn.

Listening to your body is not difficult. You were born knowing the language and hearing the communication. As an adult you may simply be out of practice tuning in. My encounter with Mr. Nagai in the following story reminded me how easy listening internally can be when there's no mental resistance.

Top Gun

On my first day working at a new resort, I saw the solitary name, Nagai, on the appointment roster for a ten o'clock massage. I presumed he was a tourist from Japan and started mentally brushing up on my college Japanese. I couldn't remember the phrasing for, "Please breathe deeply", or "Is this too much pressure?" but I figured I could get my point across and ask him the words I didn't know.

The man who appeared at 9:58 that morning stood over 6 feet tall with handsome salt and pepper hair. I introduced myself and he stuck out his hand, saying "I'm Jim Nagai" with a broad Texan drawl. I hadn't met a Japanese-Texan before. I quickly learned he was an Air Force pilot of the *Top Gun* variety, forty-two years old, and had never had a massage before.

As I worked on his back and shoulders, I could feel him focusing on what I was doing, *feeling* how it felt. I asked him to breathe deeply and notice how much better the tight spots felt when he breathed into the area than when he held his breath. To my surprise, he took a few deep breaths and his muscles fell loose. He *got* it immediately.

I told him I was impressed at how quickly he could drop his tension and that he broke the stereotype of "uptight military guy." He laughed and told me he'd undergone intensive training in flight school, sitting in a chair for countless hours strapped to electrodes and monitors. He had to learn to tighten his muscles at will in order to elevate the blood pressure in his head so he wouldn't black out while making turns at 9 Gs![6] He also told me about the flight suit that high performance pilots wear that has air bladders in the thighs to squeeze blood back up into the head for the same reason. I laughed at the thought of the U.S. Military using fancy technology to teach people to be tense. Nevertheless, they were training him to *listen* to his body.

He was as fascinated by the thought of using his attention to relax as I was at the thought of using the attention to tense up. He had already re-established the link between his conscious will and his body in flight school, so making the switch from consciously tightening to consciously relaxing his muscles was easy for him. He was attentive and curious, and he already knew how to listen to his body, so my suggestions didn't frighten him

---

6   G-force is a measure of gravitational pull. Nine Gs is a pressure nine times stronger than we'd feel at sea level.

at all. It helped that he didn't seem to have massive emotional defenses, but maybe he had worked through those, too. Mr. Nagai showed me how easy it can be to release tension when the will isn't resisting. Then all I had to do was explain how it was in his best interest to let the energy flow and he did the rest. It was a pleasure to feel him *getting* it.

Wouldn't it be great if we all were taught to recognize the tension in our bodies and work with it as we grow up? Imagine classes in high school, or even grade school, that teach kids how to feel the tension in their bodies and how to let it go. That would be fantastic. Monitors and electrodes would be unnecessary, especially with kids who haven't already severed that mind-body link. I've taught my own kids to stay tuned in, and I've gone to their schools to talk with their classmates about breathing and listening internally. It's really not as far-out as it might seem at first, and I bet integrating those concepts would help kids stay healthier throughout their lives.

When you go for a medical diagnosis, initially you are asking a doctor to listen to *your* report of *your* physical symptoms and give *his* or *her interpretation* of what you report. No matter how skilled or experienced the doctor, he makes your diagnosis based on limited information. Down the road of illness, the doctor will use her experience and training to interpret specific test results. By the time medical tests indicate there's something wrong, your body is significantly out of balance. You can see the benefit of consulting your body long before it gets to that point.

Your body knows *all* of what's going on in its systems at every moment. It knows whether you've rested enough, drunk enough water, and breathed enough for its specific needs that day, week, year. It knows if you are carrying a load of undigested resentment, fear, or grief. And it will tell you to "slow down," "drink more water," or "take a walk in the woods"—if that's what you need—before the imbalance becomes a serious dis-ease. It does not speak in terms of "radiation poisoning" or "heart disease" but it will tell you, "this job is killing me," or "I'm stiff and dehydrated and need to take a break," long before your condition becomes serious. Your body will tell you what decisions to make, how to take care of yourself—even what people to hang out with—if you consistently practice "trusting your gut."

In the following story, working with Sasha was a wonderful reminder for *me* of how clearly the body communicates when it trusts that someone is listening. In this case, it was her body and both of our trust.

I Can Put my Finger on It

I used to go to a monthly forum that gave people the opportunity to try out alternative healing modalities for free. All kinds of far-out and not-so far-out people would show up to get worked on, promote their business, exchange ideas, and eat a healthy meal together. First we would hold hands in a circle and do a little easy tai chi; then those doing the work would introduce themselves and explain what kind of work they did (Reiki, aromatheraphy, foot reflexology, etc.) and we would break into informal groups.

I had come with my 85-yr-old friend, Gerard, who did energy work. Gerard had learned to clear energetic blockages from a person's auric field by passing his hands a few inches away from the body and culling out energy that feels unhealthy. He variously describes his sensations of blocked energy as "thick," "heavy," "hot," "prickly" or "stringy," while healthy auric energy feels "smooth," "satiny" or "clear". In my experience, Gerard's treatments feel wonderfully refreshing and soothing, and he had taught me to do them as well.

Gerard and I were working together at one table when Sasha, a woman in her late thirties, 5'8," and a robust 190 lbs. approached for a treatment. With a few words of introduction she lied down (fully clothed) on the table. As Gerard began to pass his hands over her, she said she could feel what he was doing even though he never touched her. He invited me to give it a go and I made a few passes over her body the way he had taught me. After that, I felt called to touch her because I felt at this point there was more work to be done in her body than out in the aura. I asked her if I could do a little bodywork. She agreed.

I massaged where I felt blockage in the liver area and in the lower abdomen and then asked Gerard to go over those areas one more time. Sasha said she felt better and got up off the table. I then took her over to a corner of the room for additional privacy and said quietly, "I feel that there's something in your left breast. I didn't want to say anything in front of all those people. I've never done anything like this before but I get the impression I'm supposed to push my thumb into your left breast."

She looked me in the eye and said, "I trust you. Go for it."

I firmly pressed my thumb into the spot on her left breast that was calling me to do so. I felt what I would describe as a sickly green energy ooze down my legs and into the earth. It felt yucky going down but wonderful to have out. We looked at each other, wide-eyed. "What did you just feel?" I asked.

"It felt like green slime dripping down and out of my body," she said. My eyes widened. She continued, "I had a biopsy done on that breast, right there. A few days ago." She pointed to the spot I had pushed.

"Oh God," I said. "I'm sorry. I shouldn't have done that."

"No, I think you did the right thing. You asked first," she assured me. "It had been hurting and now it feels better."

I told her I had felt the same thing: like green slime oozing down and out of my body.

It felt strange doing something so socially unorthodox. But the intuitive message I got was so clear, I would have felt worse not following it. At least I had to ask Sasha if she was open to trying it. She could certainly have said "no". And what we felt was not physical pus draining down our legs and into the floor, it was energy flowing down and out.

I ran into Sasha at a store a week or so later. She was excited to see me. She said she had gone to the doctor and he had found an abscess. One of the biopsy stitches had gotten infected and it had already begun to drain. He said he would have put her on antibiotics, but by then it had drained enough that he felt it wasn't necessary. It was now completely healed.

Physical pain can become emotional torment and vice versa. It's all part of the same continuum. Dr. Deepak Chopra explains that what we call physical, psychological, emotional phenomena are all energetic manifestations vibrating at different rates[7]. Whether we call it physical or emotional or mental, it's all the same stuff—energy.

If you notice feeling down or vaguely resentful, there's a good chance there are deeper issues waiting in the wings. If watching a sad movie triggers a huge crying fit, or you blow up at your child for spilling a glass of milk, pay attention to these outbursts. Your psyche is communicating with you. You can bet there are pent up emotions waiting to be released. If left to compound, those emotions will get heavier and denser, and solidify into physical problems. Start to recognize your body's physical tugs about latent emotional issues, such as tight back muscles or an achy feeling in your chest. Create an opportunity to be alone—out in nature, or even in your car—when you can allow yourself to cry or laugh or scream or sigh to release emotional build-up. This may seem weird or scary at first but it gets easier with practice. It's way better than letting the emotional backlog fester and grow.

In the words of psychologist and author Alice Miller, "The truth about our childhood is stored up in our body, and although we can repress it, we can never alter it. Our intellect can be deceived, our feelings manipulated and conceptions confused, and our body tricked with medication. But someday our body will present its bill, for it is as incorruptible as a child, who, still whole in spirit, will accept no compromises or excuses, and it

---

7   Chopra, Deepak. *Quantum Healing* (Bantam, New York, 1989)

will not stop tormenting us until we stop evading the truth."[8]

This "bill" Miller talks about is one of the body's most precious gifts. It is the symptoms that call your attention to an emotional problem. It is the pain that forces you to see the truth of your experience and to heal through it. While you may not be able to change the facts of your experiences, you can alter your reactions to them. You can rewrite your stories so they *feel* different. You can look at your parents and recognize them for the wounded people they were, forgive, and let go. More than likely they were doing the best they knew how. They were masters in the making, just like you. You can forgive them and forgive yourself. You can allow your emotions to flow through you and out, thereby draining the emotional charge from your memories. You can let love flow in to replace the hurt and fear. It simply takes the decision to change and the will to allow it.

A lot of the tension I feel in my client's bodies is "physio-emotional" pain. It is exactly the bill Miller is talking about and it starts out as stuck emotional energy and accumulates as tension until it overflows as physical and/or emotional symptoms. The body finally expresses a problem physically because the mind (psyche) has not allowed the emotions to express consciously. Like a wave unable to roll through, the energy can build up and do damage. As undigested emotional experiences accumulate, so does the energetic sludge or resistance that manifests as what we call "stress." Long-term physical stress becomes what I call "energetic armor." We will discuss both of these further in the next chapter.

---

8   Miller, Alice. *The Drama of the Gifted Child* (Basic Books, New York, 1996)

As you are learning to listen to your body, you may find it easier to "listen" to the bodies of others at first. In a few moments you can gather volumes of raw data on someone by paying attention to how he moves, the look of his skin, and where he puts his attention.

Picture the cell phone salesman I met last week. You probably know someone just like him. He is a man of about 35 who moves and talks fast, breathes shallowly, and carries visible tension in his neck and shoulders. I figured from his build and agility that he played sports when he was younger, perhaps still does something physically strenuous on weekends, probably works out some at a gym, and yet carries thirty extra pounds. He focuses completely on what is in front of him to the exclusion of what's going on in his body. When I extrapolated the pattern further, I guessed he eats fast, works too much, and generally overdoes it. I tactfully asked him and he confirmed it.

I wasn't reading his external "body language" (posture, facial expressions and such) as much as my intuitive "take" on his energy and how it does or does not flow in his body. Many people who pay attention to bodies can tell at least this much about a person after a brief encounter.

Pay attention on this level to three people you observe today and see what information you can gather from your first impressions. You are not judging anyone, just exercising your intuition and observational skills. If you can, ask questions to verify your impressions. To build confidence in your intuitive listening to bodies, continue observing strangers or people you don't know well. Sometimes you can dig further to see if your intuitive "take" was right. The more you observe and pay attention to feedback, the more you learn how to read the clues. As you learn from observing other people you will find you are learning about yourself in the process.

Just as it's often easier to see patterns in other people, it's often easier to love someone else than it is to love yourself. The trick is to extend the love that you feel toward others to include yourself. Maybe you didn't get touched well when you were young. Maybe you were touched violently or not at all. Your caregivers may have simply passed down the harsh treatment they received as children. Or they didn't realize how much you needed to be hugged and touched with gentleness and love. But you can now rewrite those harsh stories with kinder, gentler ones. You can give yourself the care and tenderness you didn't get back then. You can teach yourself that you are worthy of loving care by doing loving things for yourself.

Self-love is an attitude followed up by loving action. One follows the other in a continuous cycle. You can practice receiving loving touch and attention by getting a massage. See if the next time someone hugs you, you can pause and really take it in. Even if you don't completely believe it, do it anyway. Think of your body as a miraculous creation, capable of withstanding so much and performing so well. Start to see your scars as simply signs of past pain or injury—and evidence that you have healed. My mom used to say, "I'm proud of my gray hairs, I've earned every one." You can come to see anything you don't *like*—such as excess fat, pain, or disease—as simple evidence of past experience and/ or current imbalance and realize that you have a choice in your attitude about it. Non-judgementally *accepting* the issues you carry in your body is the first step toward healing them. Shifting to a loving, accepting attitude toward your wounds can initiate the healing changes that you have wanted all along.

Love That Pain

Physical pain is part of the human experience—and it is not inherently a bad thing. Its primary function is to alert you to a problem. Like a fire engine siren, it is loud and irritating specifically so you can't ignore it. If you simply medicate away minor pain, that's like shutting the windows on the fire next door so you don't hear the sirens. That doesn't change the problem that underlies it—the fire's coming. Pain initially gives you the opportunity to heal yourself before a problem gets huge. Without it, you would get no warning that there is a problem until you collapse from overload. Once you see pain for what it is—a wake up call—you won't suffer *over* your suffering. The pain won't pain you. You can appreciate it for the intense, annoying and effective communication that it is and take action before it becomes intense enough to stop you in your tracks.

In the 1970s, we often heard the term *psychosomatic*[9]. An illness was labeled "psychosomatic" when the doctors could find nothing physically wrong to explain the physical pain and other symptoms people felt. It's "all in your head", they'd say, "a figment of your imagination", "not real." People suffering pain that couldn't be explained were called hypochondriacs and seen as whiners or crackpots. The prevailing medical attitude was, "If medicine doesn't understand it or if science can't measure it, it's purely imagined, it doesn't exist." Emotions, emotional pain and all the subjective and imprecise parts of our experience were considered irrelevant to our medical profile. It was hugely

---

9   *Psycho-* meaning 'of the mind, mental' and *-somatic* meaning 'of the body, physical'.

frustrating when, imagined or not, we hurt. That artificial distinction—either "physical and therefore real" or "mental and therefore unreal"—made it hard to look at the whole problem, which usually has physical, mental, emotional, and spiritual components.

Fortunately, a humbler wisdom is seeping into medical culture that acknowledges the divine—perhaps *scientifically* unknowable—and multidimensional nature of our wonder-full selves. Medical experts are finally looking beyond rigid structural models to see the human body as more than just a collection of mechanical systems. They are increasingly looking at the whole person for explanations for pain and suffering, even when those explanations don't fit with conventional medical treatment. Doctors are finding the courage to say, "I don't know. We don't fully understand this yet." They now recognize that just because there is no medical explanation for a person's symptoms doesn't mean they are a figment of the imagination. And patients are finding the courage to take responsibility for their own healing and look for their own answers. This includes venturing into murky, uncharted emotional waters and developing a relationship with the intuitive. Often the intuitive explanation is the best one.

I love this! Just the other day a friend of mine, a beautiful operating-room nurse, was medically diagnosed with "Broken Heart Syndrome". She had recently given up the home she loved, had marital strife, her twelve-year-old son shattered his leg in a kite-sailing accident, and she was feeling her life spinning out of control. After a day of kayaking and feeling chest pains, she went to the emergency room and was then airlifted to the big medical center on the next island. She underwent two days of intensive and invasive diagnostic procedures and was finally diagnosed with *stress cardio myopathy*, otherwise officially known as "Broken Heart Syndrome." It is described in medical literature as "a sudden temporary weakening of the heart (in her case, an enlargement of the left ventricle) triggered by emotional stress."

I asked her what she had been feeling. She said, "I was quivering inside feeling the pain in my child. I felt my heart was crushed. So much had happened recently, my son's accident was just the straw that broke the camel's back. Everything was all connected." For years medical researchers noted physical symptoms like my friend was having and traced them back to the emotional stress they had felt beforehand. The medical evidence overwhelmingly shows emotions, "stress", causing physical reactions such as adrenaline enlarging portions of the heart. The good news not only is that my friend is going to be fine, but that medicine is officially opening its eyes to the emotional components of physical problems! Emotional pain and physical pain are part of the same continuum.

The more you pay attention to and respond to your body's gentler signals, the less your body must raise its voice by screaming with intense or debilitating symptoms. Pain and other physical symptoms are primarily your body's way of calling your attention to a problem. You can get used to pain, or the wires can get crossed and it may become linked with pleasure, but by definition, pain is supposed to be unpleasant so that you will *pay attention* to it.

If you put your hand on a hot stove, the painful burning sensation is the body's signal to get your hand out of there. If it hurts to step on a sprained ankle the body is saying, "This has not healed enough to bear weight." Your body will present increasingly annoying or painful symptoms until you pay attention and do what it is telling you to do. Once you realize this, your response to pain changes from, "How can I get rid of this immediately?" to "What is my body telling me now?" Once you begin to recognize pain as your ally, a key part of your body's vocabulary, you can use it as a vehicle to greater self-awareness and improved overall health.

If you are already in heavy physical and/or emotional pain, all you can do is start where you are. Each deep breath is a courageous demonstration to yourself that you can move through it. As you practice, your ease and confidence will grow. Learning your body's communication may mean digging layer by layer into long-held physical and emotional patterns. That's okay. That's your work to do. As you clear away one layer of pain and discomfort, a deeper layer of pain may surface. That's okay. It may feel like your body screams louder (presents more intense symptoms) as you heal, but it could also be that your internal hearing is improving.

Discovering deeper layers of dis-ease is not to be confused with a "healing crisis". A healing crisis happens when your body is channeling all its resources into overcoming illness and symptoms peak. During a bout with the flu, for example, the healing crisis occurs when the fever spikes, aches and pains hurt the most, and you can do nothing but lie there and ride it out. It feels like you're getting worse when in fact your body is heating up literally to burn out the virus. Despite how it might feel, that's exactly what your body needs to heal fully.

An emotional healing crisis can take the form of a tantrum, a bout of depression, or a fit of rage, for example, but the effect is the same. It's as if something has to be blown out, energetically. While it feels terrible in the moment, a tantrum is an effective way to release a lot of pent-up emotion, fast. While a bout of depression is no fun, it's your psyche's way to hold your personality down while it heals deep psychological pain.

So what about the unexpressed emotions stored in *your* body? What might you be holding onto? How do you get to those feelings and call them forth for release? What might happen when you do? That's what we'll look at in the next three chapters.

CHAPTER 5—

Stress, the Body's "NO"

Stress happens when your mind resists what is...
The only problem in your life is your mind's
resistance to life as it unfolds.

~ Dan Millman

Stress. We hear so much about it. But what is it exactly? Stripped of details, it is some part of us saying "no" to something. In that "no" is resistance, a physical contraction, a constriction, a pulling away from, a negative thought, and an emotional aversion. In the process, energy and breath slow or shut down. No, means "energy doesn't flow." Stress is a useful and necessary thing—like when a child puts his hand near fire, feels the increasing heat edge toward pain, and withdraws his hand. The pain response tells the child "no" and he learns to avoid fire. Sometimes we need to learn what to avoid in order to know what to move toward. But we overdo "no". We accumulate resistance, we stay restricted and experience that shut-down in all the ways we label "stress."

As we are growing up, every time we want to shout or punch or cry but stop ourselves to avoid criticism—we are saying "no" to part of ourselves. Every time we feel blamed, unseen, unloved, abandoned, unappreciated, ugly, unworthy, or lacking, we experience resistance, constriction, and "no". We constrict and restrict our breath. We go through our lives accumulating "no" in our minds and in our bodies and yet wonder how we got so "stressed out."

Fight or Flight

You have probably heard people talk about the "fight or flight" response. It is an animal's coordinated set of physical responses to a perceived threat—the active defense choices. Picture a cat sleeping peacefully. Suddenly, a barking dog charges up to it, ready to attack. Immediately the cat's brain signals for certain chemical changes to take place within its body. Blood races to its muscles. It springs up. Digestion stops so more blood and energy can flow to the limbs; breathing, blood pressure, and pulse increase. Adrenaline surges through its brain and muscles and its body is ready to defend itself to the bitter end. The dog attacks, the cat runs. If cornered, the cat will hiss and spit and its hair will stand on end to seem more formidable. The cat will fight if it has to, but prefers to escape because there is less likelihood of getting hurt (or killed) if there is no physical confrontation.

Afterwards, the cat will pant and then breathe more slowly to recover the oxygen it lost from fast breathing and reset its metabolism. It will slink away, lick its wounds and rest until it has recovered its strength. The cat knows it is dangerous to face another threat before it has recovered from the last one and it takes time to replenish and rebalance its body. This entire sequence--fight or flight plus recovery--serves to maximize an animal's chances for healthy survival.

Animals also have passive defenses. Especially young or weak animals tend to freeze or faint in defense if fighting or fleeing doesn't seem like a viable option. Imagine a baby deer meets a bear. The fawn isn't fast or strong enough to take on the bear so it shuts down its breathing and freezes so the bear will lose interest and move on.

Human animals have the same response options to a threat: fight, flight, freeze or faint—and go through the same physical sequences. As children, if we saw bullies coming after us, our hearts would race, our digestion would shut down, and blood would rush to our limbs. We'd feel a surge of adrenaline. We might try to hide (freeze) at first, but if they found us we'd run (flee). If we got caught we would fight back or go limp (faint), depending on which seemed safest. A drunken father or an enraged mother might have felt as dangerous as a wild animal. As children though, our options to run away or fight scary adults were limited so we shut down in some way, stuffing down intense emotions as part of the physical response. When we feel we can't flee or fight our way out of a bad situation, we hold our breath or breathe minimally and freeze, hoping the threat will pass us unscathed. We internalize the fear without release or recovery.

In nature, animals don't seem to resent being attacked. They will learn from an attack and try to avoid it in the future but there's no resentment, no grudge, no lingering negative charge. The loser of a fight will flap its wings, cry out, or in some way physically release the built-up energy as part of recovery. Then it's over. But our thoughts and judgments anchor the negative

SADLY, JOE PENGUIN WAS FAILED BY HIS "FIGHT OR FLIGHT" RESPONSE

charge into our bodies . We think, This shouldn't have happened to me! or I deserve this punishment because I'm unworthy. The resentful/angry/sad thoughts become feelings as they materialize in our bodies. Tension that begins as a simple physical response to a threat becomes stress as worries about past and future anchor it into our bodies.

As adults, while we may not face physical attack anymore, we may fear losing our home, our job, our family; being hurt, abandoned, ridiculed, or humiliated. Our bodies still react in fear as if they were physically threatened, but often we're just reacting to fearful thoughts. Because there's no attacker to fight or flee, there's no physical release of the stress and the fearful energy gets internalized. Our emotional and physical reactions to a stressor--anything that threatens us and anything we resist--are inextricably bound together. And unless we learn new reaction patterns and release the stress, as adults we respond to a perceived threat emotionally and physically as if our lives were at stake.

Another difference from our wilder animal brethren is that we habitually do not take the time to rest and recover between threatening situations. We skip the recovery phase and go directly from one stressful task to another. We get so caught up in our fearful thoughts we don't tell our bodies that the threat isn't real. We get accustomed to the fearful contraction and take it as normal. Our hard-wired defenses are meant to protect us from harm, but when we don't allow the cycle to complete itself by letting go of the energy and resting, we wind up accumulating the stress in our bodies and they begin to break down because of it.

Many of the people I work on have been living in constant flight/flight/freeze mode for years. They're just regular busy people – parents, sons, daughters, workers, drivers, artists, athletes – working through the trials and challenges they face daily. They've been so constantly beset by threats and stresses in their lives that the pattern of shallow breathing, limited digestion and tight muscles has become their normal state. They are so accustomed to internalizing the adrenaline rush that they hardly notice it. They watch violent movies or do dangerous sports to give them an extra "hit" of adrenaline that they can control. In nature, an animal goes into flight or fight mode only when necessary and then it releases the energy. Humans get into the habit and do it for "fun" and then wonder why they wear out so fast.

To bring this into your body, now, picture Sandra, a computer sales representative, at work. She gets a phone call from an angry client complaining that the computers he ordered didn't arrive on time. While she's dealing with that, her boss interrupts to discuss last quarter's flagging sales figures. Then the school nurse calls to say her son got hurt playing soccer at recess; his tooth got knocked loose and his mouth is bleeding. But she has an important presentation to give in twenty minutes at another office and she can't pick him up just then. Her life is not threatened, but her job and her child are in subtle danger. Her breathing becomes more shallow, her digestion stops, and her body shifts into overdrive in reaction to the stress. She pulls more energy into her head to help make split-second decisions. She tells the school nurse she'll be there as soon as she can. She calls her husband to see if he can get their son. He doesn't pick up the call.

She has fifteen minutes before the sales meeting: she has to prepare her materials and leave. She realizes she hasn't had lunch, so she downs the rest of the cold coffee on her desk and hopes that will carry her through the meeting. The presentation doesn't go well. The boss warns her to focus harder. She finally gets through to her husband, who picks up the hurt child, but they're both mad at her for not being available. Her head starts pounding. She thinks about eating something but her stomach is so knotted she can't eat. She makes a few more calls and leaves her office. On the drive home, she realizes she's exhausted, but there's another child to pick up from karate, dinner to make, and homework to help with. She can't let down. She grabs some fast food on the way to the dojo, and it doesn't digest. After racing through the tasks of the evening, she takes some pain medication and falls into bed exhausted, only to get up and do it again the next day.

Okay. Check yourself. After reading that did your shoulders tense up? Are you breathing fast? Is your chest tight? (I certainly got tense writing it.) Can you feel the "no!" in your body? And not only was this not life-threatening, it didn't even happen to you! So, right now, while you're still feeling wound up from that stressful passage, here's an opportunity to practice a new pattern. Tell yourself it was only an exercise and that it didn't happen to you. You're safe. Take a breath. Drop your attention into your shoulders and belly and let the energy pass through your body without holding on to it. Breathe deeper. Smile. That's all you have to do and it's very powerful.

Especially with the fast pace of modern life we need to give ourselves time to recover and reset. We need opportunities to "process" the emotions that we stuff down in times of crisis, to pant, lick our wounds, and rest, so to speak. In order to function best, the body needs down time to balance the effects of accumulated stress and too much doing. We need to balance the "no" with "yes," exhale with inhale. We need to breathe and reset after a confrontation – even if it only happened mentally – and we continually need to reassure ourselves that we're okay.

In the next few days, see if you can notice when fear winds you up, how tension and stress build in your body throughout your day. When you do, pause a moment, breathe the energy through your body and let go of it. If you talked yourself into anxiety, take a moment to talk yourself out of it. You can shift from passively internalizing the energy to actively (gently) discharging it. It only takes a decision that you will do it. That's the mental step. Breathing is the physical step. It's free, it's portable, and no one even needs to know you're doing it! Take another full breath now.

☯

It is my impression that virtually any organ or system in the body can be used by the mind as a defense against repressed emotionality.

~John Sarno, M.D.

Emotional Armor

Your body is wonderfully efficient. Once it understands it is being asked to be defensive most of the time, it will oblige by finding an efficient way to be defensive. It does this by building an energetic shield that goes up when you feel attacked so that your body is ready to meet a new threat at any moment. Then, over the years, your body reinforces this defensive shield in the way that an oyster builds a pearl, layer by layer, in response to an irritating, invading grain of sand. The net result is a kind of "energetic armor" that serves to block out unwanted emotions. Leaving the armor in place feels like less work than constantly taking it off, examining how much of it you really need, and putting only the necessary bits back on. It also feels safer. You grow accustomed to the burden of the armor, finding ways to work around and despite it. Most of the time, you forget it's there but when pain reminds you, you find you don't know how to take it off.

You grow up meeting threatening situations. This is how you learn to manage yourself in the world. Imagine having to walk home knowing the school bully is laying in wait for you on the way. You feel the fear surge through your body. Your shoulder, neck, and jaw muscles tense up and you get a knot in your stomach. You're in flight or fight mode. The bully may never materialize, but your body has gone through the motions anyway. Now imagine yourself balled up as your father or older sister comes at you for a tickle attack. Tickling can be fun or an agony (or a bit of both), but you tighten your muscles to ward it off in any case, and the ticklish holding pattern can persist for decades. Imagine insults from a teacher or a parent raining down on your head and shoulders like blows; picture what that does to your posture and imagine your tension level. Think about where all that negative energy goes.

These are all instances where the muscles naturally tighten against a threat even though the threat is not literally life-threatening. They are all "no"—which if not a problem in itself. The problem is not giving yourself the benefit of the recovery phase to balance it out. Then there's physical abuse, sexual assault, traumatic injury, and illness—all of which "hit" you on physical and emotional levels simultaneously. The armor can have several complex layers to it. If you haven't digested and released the traumatic emotions, you still carry the energy in your body, in your tissues, and you experience it first as tightness or "stress." Over time, that energy accumulates until you experience symptoms, whose function is to call your attention to healing.

Un-shouldering emotional armor that has built up over years may happen bit by bit. The process of breathing deeply and allowing emotion to flow again may feel strange as the old muscular habits are challenged, but in time, and with practice, your body will be able to move faster, easier and more freely. As you release the emotional energy you've been holding onto, you may find extra layers of sadness or self-recrimination as you realize the extent of your self-imposed burden and what you have suffered with it. Each step in the process gives you confidence and inspiration to continue. And there are short-cuts.

A healer or someone who has been through the process can help you discover the shape of your metaphorical armor and help undo the buckles. When the mind has set up defenses to keep awareness out of the body and away from troublesome emotions, an intuitive healing approach can help bypass the mental defenses and go directly to where the emotional energy sits in the body. It can find the "no" and initiate a "yes" to balance it out.

The following story shows what an intuitive approach to unbuckling the armor looks like. I often tell it to illustrate how a person can have pent-up emotion long overdue for release and that the release can be quick and easy. I also tell it when I feel a person is overall so emotionally pent-up, he simply needs a good cry as a first healing step.

The Man with Sobbing Shoulders

One day a strapping 34-year-old by the name of Patrick came to see me for a massage. His new wife had insisted he get a massage, knowing he could use some bodywork after a hectic wedding. He had had one or two massages before, and no recent surgeries or other health concerns.

As I began working on his back, my hands kept coming back to his shoulders. I rested my hands there to listen more closely. After a few moments, the impression was so strong I said, "I feel sobbing here, in your shoulders. You know how your shoulders heave when you cry really hard? It feels as if they're frozen mid-sob. It feels like crystalline tears stuck in the muscles."

He lifted his head out of the face cradle to reply, "I haven't cried since I was sixteen."

"Well," I asked, "What happened when you were sixteen?"

"That's when my parents got divorced," he said.

Aha, I thought, *that's it.* I felt an extra surge of energy in my body—confirmation. "So you never had a chance to cry?" I said.

He said, "Guys in my family aren't allowed to cry."

"Well, I won't tell anyone in your family!" I said. "You're on vacation. You'll probably never see me again. This is your chance to unblock the energy that's been stuck there all these years. I bet you'll feel a whole lot better."

I continued working, pushing on the energetic knots in his muscles and trying to ease them into letting go of the emotional load they carried. I was looking for an opening in his subconscious will. When someone's will is fixed on holding in emotional pain—for whatever reason—I've found that physical pressure alone cannot force the muscles to release the tension pattern. Patrick's mind wasn't allowing his muscles to let go but he had no conscious awareness of how to do it. He needed to open his inner door for himself and I intuitively searched for words that would knock in just the right way.

"Divorce is a raw deal for everyone, but especially for the kids," I said. "Kids blame themselves for the breakup. As if you were somehow better, your parents would have stayed together. Talk about ripping your whole world apart..." I felt compassion for the boy in pain and kept working.

Within a few minutes, he started to cry. Powerful, heartfelt sobs shook out in waves. These tears were eighteen years overdue. He eventually soaked the covering of the face cradle. I kept quiet and let the energy pass on through.

When he turned over so I could work on his frontal side, I noticed that his face looked raw and new, like a bud emerging from a husk. People often look like they've just awakened from sleep when they come out of the face cradle but this was more dramatic than that. He wasn't self-conscious, just busy integrating the experience.

I kept thinking about the latest version of Disney's "The Parent Trap" and suggested he rent a copy. (It is about divorce/familial separation from the child's perspective, and it always makes me cry even though my parents are still married.) He said it was "funny that I should mention it," as he had been about to rent it the week before. I figured he had more divorce-related feelings to work through —anger, fear, sadness—and tears to shed. Seeing the movie might bring up different issues and help him release more of those overdue tears.

When he got up from the massage table he looked as if the weight of the world had been lifted from his shoulders. His body had been ready to let go of it, even though his conscious mind wasn't aware of it. It was the combination of talk and understanding, intention, and intuition that made it happen. I never heard whether he rented "The Parent Trap." But I do know that helping him feel the connection between his tight shoulders and those unshed tears was the most profound thing I could have done for him that day.

I tell this story a lot. Even a diehard skeptic will acknowledge the relief of crying out pent-up sadness and grief. Telling a similar story creates an opening. It serves as a roadmap into emotional territory where a person may never have ventured before. Then too, the *way* I tell it lets people know that not only am I not going to judge them for their reactions, I'm going to encourage them to breathe—maybe even have a good cry like the guy in the story. In fact, in the next story, Patrick's tears helped catalyze a release for Carrie. His story showed her how it could be done and gave her permission to let down her own defenses.

❧

The Wounded Wife

Carrie, another 34-year-old, and mother of three young children, had arrived for her poolside massage wearing a wet, sandy bathing suit. It was windy and she said she was cold. I wrapped her in several towels and worked on one small, exposed part of her body at a time. I soon saw that she wasn't getting anything out of the massage. She criticized whatever I did as too hard, too slow, or "not right." Finally, with eight large towels covering her and nothing I did to her satisfaction, I realized it wasn't just about the wind—or me. She had all her defenses up and would not let anything I did penetrate. She had shut down. I had no idea why. In fact, when she had talked with me an hour earlier to set up the massage, she had seemed eager and pleased at the prospect, open. I was baffled by the change.

I paused for a moment to tune in to my intuition and and felt pent-up sadness and frustration—like she needed to cry. I got the idea to tell her about Patrick's shoulders and asked her if I could tell her a story. She nodded. Before I even finished telling it, she started crying. She told me that her husband had just hurt her feelings a few moments before she lay down for the massage and she was still upset. They were on a special vacation, away from the kids, and she had wanted this trip to

Hawaii to be full of romance and reunion. He hadn't noticed all the special ways she had tried to make herself beautiful for him and to make the trip romantic. Instead, he had been acting cold and aloof, barely speaking to her most of the time.

After listening to her story, I said, "It's not really *him*, is it? The pattern goes deeper than that. Did your father treat you the same way?" I paused. As those words left my mouth goose bumps bloomed on my arms—*bingo*, my physical-intuitive signal for truth. "Are these painful feelings now, of not being seen as beautiful and valuable, what you also felt with your father growing up—especially as you were growing into womanhood?"

She smiled up through her tears and nodded.

I explained how those are common issues between fathers and daughters and how a woman's choices in men often reflect those issues. Specifically, women repeatedly choose men who are emotionally unavailable and don't seem to appreciate their womanhood because that's the model they learned from their fathers during adolescence. They keep giving themselves opportunities to work it out for the better. Fathers (men) can have mixed and conflictive feelings about their daughters growing into womanhood and often respond by pulling away emotionally. Carrie said that that was her experience with her father: he pulled away emotionally.

I could feel her getting excited by the connections she was making. Energy was zipping around her body and she was getting warmer. I told her about a book,[10] that helped me understand my own patterns with men. It explained how we unconsciously choose relationships with people who can help us revisit and heal

---

10   *Getting the Love You Want* by Harville Hendricks (Henry Holt, 1988)

the dysfunction of our upbringing. By this point in the massage, I was working on Carrie's legs and she was warm enough to forego some of the towels. She said she wanted to read the book even if it was challenging. She was ready to look at her own part in the drama with her husband. I pointed out that that is the only thing she has any control over, anyway. I was excited at how receptive her mind and her body seemed to all this.

I told Carrie about a couple, friends of mine, who used to pick on each other until the bickering escalated into war. Each one could point to the other's barbs and claim the other had goaded him or her into being hurtful. When I recommended that same book to my girlfriend, both of us thought her husband was not the kind of guy who would ever read a relationship book like that. My girlfriend was so fed up with the fighting though she knew she had to do something different, even if he wouldn't participate.

In reading the book and doing some of the exercises, my friend began to see her own role in the recurring battles. When a verbal sparring session would start, she would watch herself and refrain from jabbing back. Instead of flaring into a battle each night, the bickering began to fizzle out after a few nips from him. After a couple of weeks of this, he noticed that something had changed. His sparring partner wasn't sparring with him any more. She explained what she had learned about her role in their hurtful patterns and that she had decided to change her behavior. Later that night he grabbed the book out of her hands saying, "Let me see that book!" and started to read it for himself. He *got* it, too. The new perspective and relationship tools that they got from the book catalyzed changes on many levels for them. They are now an extremely loving, married couple who are learning how to handle conflicts that come up without shredding each other in the process.

Carrie said she recognized the pattern. The steps of the hurtful dance she and her husband were doing together were probably those they learned from their respective parents. She repeatedly felt unloved because of her husband's withdrawal, then would lash out at him with criticism. His part in the dance was feeling unloved because of her criticism, then withdrawing into pain and silence. In this dance, there is no "he did it first," or "she did it first." The hurt just keeps cycling around, spiraling tighter, until one person decides to break the cycle from within. And Carrie seemed to be at the point of willingness to change.

As we talked, I felt her open up energetically. One by one, she let me take off the towels. It felt as if an old protective husk was falling away and she was intently and eagerly looking at the issues that troubled her with new understanding. I could tell I didn't need to say anything more. I felt that Spirit or her Higher Self was working to teach her something, and my role was simply to point her in a certain direction, to ground the feeling or impression with a few words and let her work it out. By the end of the massage, so much energy was flowing in her body that she was warm and no longer needed any towels.

My telling the story about Patrick gave her permission to acknowledge the pain she carried. It cut through the defensive shrewishness to the hurt underneath. And the story of how that book helped my friends was more effective at sparking her interest in it than if I had simply said, "You need to read this book." Now I'm retelling Carrie's story with the hope that the helpful cycle will continue.

I don't want to give the impression that everyone does or should cry during a massage—with me or anyone else. It's just that a lot of people are carrying the energy of unshed tears in their bodies. I tell Patrick's story most often because most people wouldn't argue with the idea that a boy of sixteen would be feeling pain during his parents' divorce and that crying is an appropriate and necessary release. Patrick didn't cry at the time of the divorce because our culture insists that expressing emotion, especially hurt, pain, sadness, or "feminine" emotions, is a sign of weakness. And he didn't want to feel weak on top of everything else he was feeling then. It is our birthright as humans to feel the full spectrum of emotions. To the extent that we can accept and allow all of them as they come up—the "dark" ones as well as the "light" ones—we are not held hostage by any of them.

If in your working life if you have become a constant producer, dwelling on the productive, masculine, *yang* side of your nature, you may have learned to push yourself, to keep going long after you know you should stop and rest. You want the light without the dark, productivity without fallow periods, and joy without sorrow. That's understandable. But life on planet Earth doesn't work that way. The wheel eventually comes full circle.

Sooner or later you have to let down, rest, grieve for your losses. It's easier and more productive in the long term if you recognize this *before* your body yanks your chain and forces you to deal with what you have been stuffing down. It's a welcome relief to embrace the feminine—the *yin*—and give yourself permission to be idle, soft, and vulnerable from time to time. This also means allowing in all your feelings including fear, sadness, anger, outrage and vulnerability. This means letting in joy. You may be so used to bonding with people in the negative—complaining and comparing how the world's done you wrong—that you have shut down your joy as well. Your working life will be more productive when it is balanced with rest, gentleness, and inspiration (*i.e. breathing in*). With practice, your rest will be more restful.

Most of the threats you meet in modern life are intellectual—a tax audit, losing your job, your spouse leaving you, financial ruin. They aren't literally life-threatening but your mind reacts as if they were and that initiates the same fear response and physical reactions. Often you are so psychologically overwhelmed by a threatening situation (and backlogged from the other stuff you haven't fully "processed") that you simply get through it as best you can. That is normal. You tense up and steel your body to protect yourself from the emotional blows and you store your feelings for processing later. But after a threat has passed, you probably don't go to your calendar and schedule in a time to process your emotions. You go on to the next challenge. As more of this energy accumulates in your body, it becomes that much harder for any feelings—your own feelings or anyone else's—to penetrate your awareness.

I notice this pattern most clearly in the bodies of police officers I've worked on. Their shoulders feel hard and impenetrable—truly like armor. They understandably want to look strong and be strong when facing down "bad guys" but the way their muscles hold emotional energy is consistently different than in other men who work out. There's more emotional content, more defensiveness—and also more caring—than I find held in the bodies of most men. I find that most people who are drawn to police work truly care about people. But the job requires them to squelch their own fear, disgust, empathy, etc. in order to do what is required in the moment. They harden themselves against the horrors of the job. And they often go from one crisis into another with no processing time in between. The job literally and physically hardens them—down to their very tissues.

Interestingly, though the firemen I've worked on also protect the public and face danger, they do not hold the defensive emotional energy or the physical —muscular/emotional—bulk policemen tend to. They don't have to deal with the same level of interpersonal stress that policemen do. Our emotional reaction to an armed assailant is very different than our reaction to a fire— though both can kill. We don't take the threat of fire personally.

A defensive mechanism becomes a problem when it persists past its use in the moment and becomes an automatic, unconscious habit. Over time, this energetic pattern, constantly reinforced by lack of breath, makes the muscles tense, sore, less efficient, and inhibits their natural, fluid functioning. Picture a heavily-armored body: overweight, with very tight neck, back and shoulders; the arms stick out slightly, and the walk is stiff. This kind of body looks and moves like a football player suited up for a game—except that the shoulder pads are built in. It's not comfortable to be in such a body. Muscles holding a lot of stale energy tend to look and feel bulky, "bound up," or "loaded". And, like an energetic force field, this armored state takes energy to maintain—it is energetically expensive and inefficient.

Imagine a house with the lights turned on and all the appliances running. There may be someone working in one or two rooms at a time, but the rest of the electric energy is blazing away, wasted. This is expensive. If you have muscles that don't "turn off" when you aren't using them, you are similarly wasting energy. You are spending energy keeping them tight. When your muscles are tense, constricted, or "pumped up" you must continually run energy to keep them that way. At rest, big, bulky muscles might look stronger than small, slender ones, but that excess muscular bulk takes energy to maintain. Toned muscles that can relax fully at rest work more efficiently.

You want to free up the old emotional energy stored in your muscles and other tissues so you can use it in better ways and have more fun. The first step is to realize how much tension you unconsciously walk around with. Once you become aware of it, you will want to dismantle the unconscious energetic defenses that don't serve you anymore. You can put this energy to better use in other ways, after all.

To see where you are running energy without needing to, try this exercise:

EXERCISE 5: Finding Your OFF Switches

Letting go of stress can be as easy as flipping a switch—if you let it be. You simply need to find the "Tension Off" switches or the "Flow On" switches. Read these instructions through first and then do the exercises with your eyes closed to feel inside more easily.

1. Loosen or take off any clothing that restricts your breathing or your comfort. Sit in a chair or lie down. Deepen your breathing.

2.   With your eyes closed, feel inside your body. Scan your neck, shoulders, and neck for tension. Move your head to help you feel which muscles are tight. Breathe into your belly, slowly and fully to let the energy flow and release the tight muscles. Imagine your muscles turning off—like turning off a light switch. You are releasing the constriction in your muscles and allowing energy to flow.

3.   If the muscles resist, talk to them. They are like soldiers you have given orders to, but then neglected to give the "stand down" order. They may have been on alert for a very long time. Ask them why they are still on duty, what they need. You may get an intuitive message like "But you told me to." or "Oh! I guess I don't need to be ON now." When neck tension makes your shoulders creep up toward your ears, for example, that's like a row of soldiers snapping to attention one by one. One muscle tenses up and then its neighbor tightens to support the first one as it tires and so on until the whole platoon is straining on alert. This happens unconsciously, brought on by thinking and concentrating hard. Breathe, smile, and ask them to stand down.

4.   Continue scanning throughout your body for tension. Check your face, your chest, your abdomen. Check your hips and legs and feet. Check your arms and hands. You can scan for tension first and then go back and release it, or you can scan and release as you go. Keep breathing fully.

5.   Acknowledge and thank your muscles for doing the great job they do. Don't berate your muscles for being tight.

They are only doing what you asked. Ask your muscles what they need. Sometimes they only need acknowledgement that they are working hard at your request. Sometimes they will tell you they need a hot bath, or a massage, or exercise, or sleep.

6. If you feel like it, get up and swizzle your hips, swing your arms; make sounds if your voice and throat feel tight. Listen to what your body asks you to do to release the tight muscles. Sometimes the muscles get frozen "ON" and you might need to jiggle something to loosen the switch so it can turn off. See if shaking your hands or wiggling your toes helps release the tension.

7. Above all, give yourself permission to relax and turn off the go-go-go. Keep breathing. Sink into the sensation of turning off.

8. When you are finished, stand up and see if you feel more fluid. See if it takes less energy to walk across the room now. I bet you'll feel more space inside your body. Play with this process and see if you can turn off lights (relax unneeded muscles) now and then throughout your day.

One last analogy: Imagine your energy as money, in units of a quarter (25¢) and each time you tighten a muscle group you deposit a quarter there and it's held there (with no interest) until you release it. Often you forget where you put your quarters as you focus on the next thing. You start your average day with a credit of $10 in quarters. If you wake up already full of chronic tension it's as if $4 worth of your daily energy assets are already frozen in your muscles. You now only have $6 of energy-quarters left to spend on your day. If you tense up as your day wears on, you're depositing even more quarters in your muscle banks; it's heavy and your liquid assets are dwindling. You can see that by evening, you're going to be exhausted-broke and lugging a burden. If you check in with your muscles now and then throughout your day (and breathe) you will release the energy (quarters) you had forgotten about and free up your energy resources for use in more productive and fun ways. Any time you feel yourself tight, you can breathe, turn off switches and release bound-up energy assets. Also do this at the end of your workday to free up energy to enjoy your evening.

When I first studied tai chi, my teacher showed the class training videos of Bruce Lee before he became a movie idol. He was lightning-fast and powerful. At rest though, his body didn't look particularly strong or fast; it certainly wasn't bulky. This surprised me because I had only seen him in films with what looked like rippling muscles. But as I watched his movies again, I realized he had such exquisite control of his body that his muscles were "on" when he needed them to be and "off" when he didn't. Seeing that movement, that strong, lightning-fast body, unhampered by the bulk so many athletes carry made a huge impression on me.

To deepen the point, my tai chi teacher also showed us a film of Tai Chi Master Cheng Man-Ching when he was roughly 80 years old. He was small and wrinkled and seemed lost in his clothing. He didn't *look* strong at all. In the film, several energetic young students attacked him at once and he flung them back like so many rag dolls. It looked effortless. He seemed to absorb the energy they directed at him and turn it back on them. Watching him move, I saw he had none of what I've been calling "body armor". He moved gracefully and efficiently with no unconscious tension to hamper his movements. He appeared to be in complete mastery over the energy that flowed through his body. His strength came from this ability to allow energy to flow through him rather than from his muscles *per se*. I could tell he had learned to live in the moment, without emotional judgment or "baggage" from past situations. I think of the time and patience and effort it took to train himself to that degree. I hold the image of his movement in my mind as an ideal to work toward. The practice starts with awareness and breath.

You can reduce your stress anytime by tuning in and processing what you feel in the moment, by saying "yes" to *what is*. Processing emotions simply means sorting through and releasing thoughts and energy that may have accumulated in your body. It's like cleaning out your desk or dumping water out of a dam that's about to burst. You don't *have* to do it but it will feel much better when you do, and it's easier to do it before the pressure builds too high. It gives you more space for new, better feelings to come in.

Go a little easier on yourself, slow down, and rest more. Yes, yes, yes! When you constantly run from one busy task to the next, you don't give yourself an opportunity to recognize if you're overloaded. When you slow down, you give yourself time to digest your experiences. Check in with yourself. Yes! How are you feeling? Take a full breath and really feel whatever that is. Yes.

Everyone encounters threatening situations and stressful periods in life. You can counter the effects of any stress building up by interrupting the cycle along the way. You can deliberately take a few deep breaths as you hang up after a tense phone call, as you watch a violent scene on TV, or exchange tense words with your teenager. This will help reverse the tension cycle. You can go so far as to close your eyes and feel how your body responded to a stressful incident. You can decide if you need to say or do anything to resolve your feelings. This is processing. It's checking in with yourself to see what, if anything needs to be attended to. Getting up to stretch and drink water after each hour spent typing at a keyboard brings energy and attention back into your body and out of your head, neck and shoulders. If you learn to release tension as it accumulates, you will be better able to respond to stressful situations as you encounter them. As your body no longer uses so much energy to maintain the defensive tension, it can use that energy in more creative and pleasurable ways. Go ahead, take a full breath now.

CHAPTER 6—

Issues in Your Tissues

Now we know that the mind and the body are like parallel universes.
Anything that happens in the mental universe must leave tracks in
the physical one.

~ Dr. Deepak Chopra

An abusive parent, a demeaning teacher, a bully on the playground—someone gave you the message, "You're not okay the way you are. You're not safe. You're not worthy." and you internalized it. That's the basic human plotline, the wound we have in common. Just about everyone has some version of it. But that's also fiction.

The truth is that you are worthy.

We wear our emotional wounds in our muscles like lint in the lining of a coat. They can accumulate and make us bulky and uncomfortable. As we can open the coat lining and clean out the accumulated lint, we can energetically go into our body and release the old emotional energy that's trapped there. When we do, we find our body looks and feels stronger and more alive.

What we experience as emotion is our body responding to our thoughts. The easy, fun thoughts flow through unrestricted—breath and muscles don't constrict in response and we go about our daily business with ease. It's the thoughts that we resist, the "no" thoughts that feel bad and cause a constrictive reaction in the body. If we stay in constriction, keep running the "no", we start down the path of dis-ease. The accumulation of this negative emotional energy is what people commonly refer to as "emotional baggage". It is the burden of unresolved or repressed thoughts that we store as tension in our bodies. It is repressed emotion.

So those "issues in your tissues" are emotions we haven't allowed ourselves to feel fully, or thoughts with a heavy emotional charge. As energetic residue in the body, they accumulate and build over time, starting first as tension and solidifying into dis-ease according to our reactions to our life experiences.

When we were little and we felt angry, we may have hit someone or lashed out in some way. If we felt sad or hurt, we may have cried. If we felt joyful, we danced or sang or jumped up and down. Perhaps we were told not to hit, or cry, or jump around but we still wanted to. We then felt conflict inside. The bad feeling from being criticized was worse than the discomfort of stuffing down our joy or sadness so we stopped dancing or crying and did what we were told. We began to suppress certain reactions (thoughts ⇒ feelings ⇒ actions) that got us into trouble, embarrassed us, or felt too *bad*. After a while it becomes a habit to stuff down emotions so we don't get teased or scolded when they showed. We began to censor our emotions and constrict the flow of their energy in order to avoid further pain and discomfort. We did this unconsciously, by holding or restricting our breath.

When traumatic things happen to us such as physical and emotional abuse, upheaval and illness, death and loss, we solidify the habit of shutting down even harder and breathing less in order to prevent ourselves from fully *feeling* painful emotions that seem too big. When we reach emotional overload, or have the thought, *I shouldn't feel that,* or *I can't let myself feel that afraid or angry or worthless,* our body responds by storing that emotional energy where we don't have to feel it—*in our tissues.*

During a crisis we need to hunker down to get through it. The crisis isn't the problem. The problem is that we don't usu- ally go back afterward to allow the feelings to move through and out; so the energy remains stuck in our body. To restore healthy balance, we need to process (let flow, or digest) the emotions we couldn't feel in the moment. Yet year after year we stuff down more feelings and our load of undigested emo- tions accumulates.

It's easier, after all, to deny painful emotions and hope they'll go away. But they don't, do they? They resurface. They come up when we least expect it, when our guard is down, or when we are so emotionally overloaded they overflow. At any moment of overload, we have two choices: we can work harder to stuff down the feelings by eating, using drugs or alcohol, watching TV, etc.—which puts off the problem but doesn't resolve it—or we can stop for a moment and give ourselves permission to feel. We can stay conscious and take a "time out" and cry, or grieve, or rage. At the very least, we can breathe and acknowl- edge that we're struggling with our feelings. This is a healthy step toward well-being.

Examples of thoughts that the body resists (a.k.a. negative emotions) are: resentment that familial burdens were heaped upon you; guilt for cheating on tests; rage at your mom for loving your brother more; relief that your friend got fired instead of you; sadness about the death of your marriage. You and every other human have experienced difficult feelings, sometimes in overwhelming amounts. Without thinking too hard you can probably list major events in your life that overloaded you emotionally. Unless you have consciously sought to release that emotional energy, chances are you still carry at least some of it. Conscious release can be as simple as recognizing that you feel angry and going for a long run or punching a pillow. The point is to recognize and *feel* your emotions in your body —not just *think* about them —and allow the energy to move through and out of your body, with breath.

You know you have unprocessed emotion if a memory still has a "charge" on it, if thinking of that situation or event still makes you feel angry or sad or joyous, even though it happened long ago. Minor or daily irritations can add additional layers to the emotional load you carry if they resonate with, or carry the same emotional flavor (vibration) as what is already there. An example would be growing up with a dad who constantly put his own needs ahead of yours. He usually arrived late, constantly kept you waiting, didn't take your needs seriously. You felt unseen, unimportant, resentful. As a consequence, as an adult, you can't stand to be kept waiting. Even when someone has a legitimate excuse for arriving late, you get upset, even enraged, at what feels like blatant disregard for your needs and your worth. If you haven't done the conscious work of disentangling your reactions to your dad's behavior, you are likely to react to being kept waiting in the same old way, even though the circumstances may be very different.

Feelings that get screened out, swallowed down, or filed for processing *later* accumulate with other such feelings. Imagine

I'LL GET YOURS, IF YOU CARRY YOUR MOTHER'S

sludgy water flowing through a filter, gradually clogging it up. Similarly, your muscles get more congested and tense as negative thought-charged energy (emotion) accumulates in your body. It restricts the clear flow of energy and creates further build-up. That energetic "sludge", depending on its concentration, can manifest as anything from simple muscular tension to life-threatening disease. Over time, your body might develop illnesses to make you stop and pay attention to the load it carries. Symptoms of disease are your body's call to heal.

The Preventive Solution

Instead of waiting until serious illness forces you to look at your emotional baggage, what if you chose to deal with it early, in a preventative way? You can listen to your everyday aches and pains for clues to emotion you have suppressed and denied. It may seem obvious that the soreness in your shoulders arises from the general stress of your daily life, but the next step is to look deeper to see if it's an indication of your unexpressed frustration, sadness or resentment. Examine the entire issue. For example, ask yourself whether the tension in your jaw arises from clamping down on all the angry feelings you haven't been willing or able to speak about. The more you practice reaching in and allowing what IS simply to be *what is*, the easier it gets. You dissipate the emotional charge, and energy flows more freely through your whole being. It simply takes practice.

You can watch the process for yourself. The next time you get really frustrated, stop for a minute and observe your breath. See if you're breathing as little as possible to keep yourself from boiling over into rage. See if you can stay conscious and deepen your breath a little more. Throw out your belly and fill your lungs. If you take deep breaths in that frustrated moment, you will allow the energy to move through you and it will dissipate rather than building up. Eventually, as you get more practice consciously feeling your frustration, you don't need to resist it and it simply flows through and out, like a wave. Another strategy you can use is to step back and see if you are over-personalizing a situation. When a situation doesn't go your way or someone treats you badly, check to see if you have done something to cause it. If so, see what you can to do fix it. If not, breathe, and realize it may not be about you at all.

☯

The pain of some experiences, like those from a car accident for example, may persist to let you know that some aspect of the wound—the emotional aspect—has not healed fully. I've worked on many people who still experience physical pain several years after a crash even though their bones and muscles have long-since mended. It's as if a negative thought, such as, *I'm a victim,* or *Bad things always happen to me,* acts as a burr which catches in the tissue and continues to irritate it. Depending on your view of who is immediately responsible for the accident, you might feel guilty, victimized, angry, vulnerable or a mix of all of these. Certainly you might feel frightened that it might happen again.

Feelings of victimization might echo back to similar feelings from childhood. Getting hit in a car accident is a common way for adults (subconsciously at least) to revisit and potentially heal childhood feelings of victimization long after they have gained "control" over most other aspects of their lives. After a car crash, a person finds himself once again in the role of "victim." The "accident" or the "other driver" is the perpetrator. The car is damaged, his body is banged up, violence has again *been done to* him without his consent. Again, he has an opportunity to react as a helpless victim or take responsibility for his reactions and heal through the experience.

As the following story illustrates, once a person sees he has a choice about how he feels, he can choose to react in a conscious way. He can ignore or deny his feelings and let them fester or he can allow himself to feel them and let them go. He can reexamine his reactions to past events and the old wounds that he still carries and apply his new insights to them. Thus a new trauma can serve as a vehicle for healing even decades-old hurt.

His Higher Calling

I remember Roger as a tall, polite man, a father, and a basketball player. He told me as he lay down on the table that he still had pain in his shoulders, left side, and lower back from a car accident he'd been in several months before. As I was feeling around in his back, I asked him the details of the accident. I felt lots of energetic knots, which I sensed intuitively as pent-up emotion. His muscles heated up as the talking and the massage brought energy flowing through them.

Roger told me he had been visiting Las Vegas on a business trip when the accident happened. A drunken teenager ran a red light and smashed into him. The muscles in his back felt physically repaired to my hands. I felt his residual pain stemmed from the unresolved, heavy emotional energy he had trapped in his muscles rather than unrepaired physical damage.

I asked Roger, "How do you feel about the accident?"

He paused, "Well, angry, I guess. That kid had no business driving like that!" His tone got angrier. "He was just a kid, sixteen. He wasn't even legal to drink. I mean, look what he did to me—and to my family. I was out of work for weeks."

"So you're angry about what that kid did to you?"

"Yeah!" His breathing sped up.

"You feel like a victim of this kid's irresponsibility?"

"Yeah."

"Tell me about this kid. Did you ever meet him?"

"Yeah, you know the story. Comes from a broken home, no dad, mother drinks, always into trouble."

"Was he upset about what he'd done?"

"Oh yeah. He's got a real mess on his hands."

"Was he sorry he hurt you? Do you think he didn't care?"

"I think he was sorry. It's just part of a long string of sorry." His breathing calmed down a bit.

"Getting drunk and crashing into another car sounds like a pretty desperate cry for help to me. You have kids, don't you?"

"Two teenage boys."

"Did you ever get drunk as a teenager?" I asked.

He didn't respond.

"Do your kids ever mess up?"

He laughed, "Yeah, all the time."

"And it makes you mad because you love them and you hate to see them blow it—hurt themselves or hurt someone else." I continued to work on those knots in his back.

"Sure it does, I love them."

"And this kid really blew it with you. I bet that screwing up is all this kid knows how to do. He gets drunk with his friends because that's all he's got. There's no dad there to tell him to knock it off or steer him in a better direction. And this time he made a *big* mistake. Do you think he got a wake up call?"

"He got it. I made sure of it," he declared. "I made sure he wasn't just going to get slapped on the hand and sent right back out there to do it again."

"That's what a loving father would do," I said gently. "do you want to know what I feel?" He nodded in the face rest. "The muscles in your back feel fine to me. Our bodies can heal even severe tissue damage in a few weeks. The tissues themselves feel repaired. What's causing you this pain is the anger and resentment you feel toward the accident and this boy who "did it to you." You feel victimized." I paused to let this sink in and feel for a reaction. "And the father in you is angry at the boy for being irresponsible. I think that's love. I can feel that you're a very loving man."

Bingo. Small snuffles and gentle sobs showed me we'd gotten through to his heart.

"Look at your life and look at that boy's." I continued, "Who's got the bigger hurts here? I'm not saying you don't have a right to feel victimized, but do you see that you could make a higher choice here? What would you say to him right now, if he were standing right here in front of you?"

He didn't reply.

"Could you forgive him? For what he did to you? Do you see that that's the way for *your* back to stop hurting? Forgive him and let the hurt go? And then forgive yourself."

I felt him nod in the head rest. He was crying in earnest at this point, releasing emotional energy.

I moved on to the knots in his lower trapesius muscles, that area I think of as where our angel wings used to be. This is where I feel conflict between a person's roles in life and their life's purpose. I felt a thrill of intuitive recognition flow through me. I said, "You have something to say to boys like him. This is the opening. For both of you. No one has ever forgiven this kid and offered him a second chance. You can do this. I can even see you running something like a boys center for troubled youth…"

He interrupted me excitely. "I already do this through my church! We have a group and I play basketball with the boys…"

"But there's more here, it's bigger." I explained about what I feel in that area between the shoulder blades, about conflict between vocation and avocation[11] and asked "What do you do for a living, your job?"

He proudly mentioned the name of a big restaurant chain throughout the Midwest as I worked on his legs. He had worked up from line employee to owning several franchised restaurants.

I asked him to turn onto his back.

"What about the boy's center idea? There's a lot more energy here in these muscles." I pointed to my own trapezius area. "When we talk about that."

"Yeah, funny you should mention it. I've always wanted to do that! But it's such a big thing. How do I start?"

"The same way you started with your restaurant franchise. One step at a time, with passion."

We talked about his church and how fulfilled he always felt when he worked with kids. His own kids were a handful, but he had more to give.

I returned to the subject of the boy who hit him. "What about that boy now? Of all the kids you've worked with, I bet he needs the fathering you have to give more than any of them. I bet that's why your paths crashed. He came along to show you how big your heart is. You can show him he's not a lost cause."

"His hearing is coming up. I was thinking of flying back out there."

"Before? In anger?"

"Yeah. Maybe now I can write him a letter. Maybe I can forgive him."

Tears squeezed out of the corners of his eyes again. I was

---

11   See the *Poet at the Foot of Kings* story in Chapter 9.

working on his shoulders now. "I can feel love here," I said.

"It feels good," he said. "God, it feels so much better than that bitterness. Yes, I can forgive him."

"Extend that circle of love you know to include him. That was Jesus' message, and Buddha's. Close your eyes. Pull him into your arms and tell him someone loves him."

"Yes."

"You're going to write him a letter?"

"I may still fly out there. But it'll be very different now. I forgive him."

"And yourself?"

"Myself? Why?"

"Haven't you been feeling pain in *your* body? Running angry, vengeful thoughts? Holding a grudge is like drinking poison and expecting the other person to die. Remove the judgment and pain disappears. Allowing love—for the other person and for the Self—to replace the anger and fear is the final stage of the healing process." I liked the way his eyes crinkled when he smiled at that.

I finished the massage. "How does your back feel?"

He stood up. "It feels great!" He reached down and gave me a hug. Then he took my hand in his and looked into my eyes. "You have a very great Faith, don't you?"

"I don't go to any church," I said.

"But you have *Faith*." His eyes were shining.

"Yes," I said. "Yes I do."

I have no doubt the story of Roger and the boy who hit him turned out well.

☯

A strictly physical approach to healing would be all we'd need if it successfully healed all physical ailments. Clearly it doesn't. Pills and surgery sometimes cause more damage than they repair. When adhering to purely physical models doesn't offer you relief, it's time to consider a more holistic approach, one that takes into consideration the emotional, psychological and spiritual aspects of your being as well as the physical. In my experience, if there is an emotional component to a physical problem that is not addressed, the physical problem persists or another problem will immediately surface in its place. If this has happened to you, read on.

Whether you see the disease-healing cycle as moving from the physical pole around through the emotional or from the emotional pole moving toward the physical, it's all part of the same cycle, the same whole-person continuum. Even Ida Rolf, the grand dame of deep bodywork whose structural approach was strictly physical, linked physical and emotional healing. She said that, "Man's emotional state may be seen as the projection of his structural imbalances." She also said, "A man crying the blues is in reality bewailing his structural limitations and failures." [12] She believed that if she improved the body's structure, the person's emotional state would improve as a matter of course. There's no question anymore that mental, emotional, and physical are connected. The question is where and how to intervene in the mind-emotion-body cycle to effect positive change.

Let's look at what happens when we shift the thought. Imagine

---

12   Rolf, Ida P., PhD. *Rolfing: the Integration of Human Structures* (Denis-Landman Publishers, 1977)

seeing two people walking hand in hand in a park. You think, "There's a couple walking together." It's a non-emotional observation. But then you realize that the man is your best friend's husband—but that's not your best friend's hand he's holding. Suddenly you judge the scene and attach emotion to it, giving it a charge, and weight. In your mind the scene was black and white until it got colored by your judgement about seeing your friend's husband with another woman. We could play this game with lots of scenes. A situation or event simply *is* until we color it with a reaction, a personal thought, or a judgement. A novel that makes you laugh and cry is affecting you emotionally, that is, through your body via your thoughts. The emotional color you give it makes all the difference as to how a thought stays with you.

Physical injuries that are black and white—that is, without emotional color—usually heal easily. For example, if you over train and tear a muscle, simple rest, basic self-care, or a trip to the physical therapist can fix it right up. Standard physical therapy includes rest, elevation, massage, strengthening exercises, ultrasound, stretching, heat and/or icing in various combinations. There is no discussion of any potential emotions involved. The thought might be, "I overused the muscle and it tore." No blame, no shame, no emotional trauma.

However, when pain persists or doesn't go away in due course, it may involve negative thoughts and/or unexpressed feelings. It's colored in a way or has a charge that makes it stick. Overusing your body usually means you ignored the message, *It's time to stop now.* You may have a perfectly good *reason* for overusing your body. It may be part of your job or your game to overuse your body, but at least some part of you resists the overuse, or it wouldn't become a problem. A thought such as, *I am sick of boxing up these walnuts*, or *I hate lifting pianos up stairs*, or *I'm going to beat him to the ball, even if it kills me*, often precedes an injury. At the time, you may not have noticed that those were your thoughts, but if you go back and look at what was going on before an injury, you often find interesting clues. Use injuries typically happen when you're not paying attention to what's going on, when you're running negative thoughts, and/or you are unhappy with the situation you're operating in.

It's understandable to want strictly physical explanations for physical problems. Who wouldn't want to be fixed easily, as if the body is a machine requiring straightforward mechanical repairs? Athletes who invest huge amounts of time and energy in their sports may treat their bodies like machines, wanting to fine-tune them to peak performance. Unfortunately this only works up to a point. Eventually these ultra-focused individuals reach a point where they can't train any harder, and injuries persist. They don't want to hear that their lives are unbalanced in some way. They just want a physical prescription that lets them get on with their sport. So their brilliant bodies help to point out the imbalance by breaking down until they get the message.

You may want a simple answer, too. But you're reading this book, so maybe the simple answers haven't been working for you.

In brief, you continue to experience physical symptoms as long as you carry the emotional "charge" or vibration associated with the original trauma. Your bones may have knitted back together and you may have regained physical function, but if you have not also released the sadness or anger or fear

123

in those tissues, your body will continue to let you know there are still issues to work on. The trick is recognizing your symptoms as an indication that there may be something non-physical to heal.

You know that who you are is much more than the physical body that you can touch, see, and smell. The package called *you* includes your physical body plus your thoughts (mental energy or mind), feelings (emotional energy), soul energy, and all the energies associated with you vibrating at different frequencies and in different dimensions. All living things run energy, much of it at vibratory rates humans cannot directly detect with their physical senses. But just as electricity existed before we understood it enough to measure it and then harness it to run our machines, human energies exist that we are only starting to understand. There are many systems that chart how and where energy accumulates in the body, a few of which I'll mention briefly.

For 3000 years Chinese medicine has been studying and working with a system of subtle energetic pathways or *meridians* that work like an invisible, energetic grid that connects all parts of the body. Chinese medicine recognizes correlations between our major organs and specific emotions. Anger is associated with or collected in the liver, grief in the lungs, fear in the kidneys, and so on. Louise Hay has come up with a wonderful reference for what might be going on at the psychological level with a physical problem in her book, *You Can Heal Your Life*[13]. It

---

13   Hay, Louise. *You Can Heal Your Life,* (Hay House, 1984)

is one of several references I consult when I am having trouble pinpointing an issue in my (or someone else's) tissues. Medical Inutitive Caroline Myss has made fascinating observations about which emotions we store in our bodies and where.

From my observations and experience, I find each of these systems to be valid on some level. They often overlap. Where there appear to be contradictions I presume different levels of energy are operating concurrently. In the *Recommended Resources* section at the back of the book, I give a list of books for further exploration into these and other approaches. You can use them as a starting point and fine-tune the information based on your body and its needs. The important thing to understand is that your health is largely determined by subtle-level energies that you cannot detect with your five senses, and that we are becoming more familiar with these energies as we evolve.

I believe our bodies are intrinsically set up to run energy in certain ways, and it's been part of our collective journey to figure out how it all works. Over the years that I've been touching people, I, too, have noticed that specific emotional energy seems to collect consistently in specific areas of the body. For example, the back muscles in the heart area seem to collect energy relating to grief, loss, and betrayal. When I say a certain part of the body "stores" or "relates to" certain emotions, somehow it's the work of that part of the body to process or store that energy. Your mind doesn't consciously choose to store emotion there, but if a certain kind of emotional energy gets stuck, that's where the body stores it until it gets released.

I use my knowledge of the physical-energetic correlations already mapped out by those who've come before me as a starting point and I then tune in with my intuition to what's in front

ISSUES IN YOUR TISSUES

of me in the moment. To stay with our heart example, I'll recall the energetic congestion I felt in the heart area of a man's back as I was working on him. I told him, "It feels stuck back here. This is where I tend to find energy relating to grief, loss or betrayal." He lifted his head and nearly shouted, "Betrayal! You mean like when my business partner of twenty-five years ups and runs off with all the profits and I can't find the guy anywhere in the country? You mean like *that*?!" Yes, that's exactly what I mean. I have come to see that "heartache" is not simply a metaphor.

Unprocessed energy from issues relating to *mother* seems to coalesce in the upper back and shoulder area at the base of the neck. This can be about one's own mother or grandmother, or the mothering role one plays with other people—even all of it combined. I remember a woman with massive tension along her whole shoulder girdle. I asked her if she wanted to explore the emotional level of her shoulder pain. She replied, "Yeah! but I wouldn't even know where to start." When I got to the spot that was screaming the loudest (exactly that "motherhood" area I'm describing, on the left (emotional) side, I pressed my thumb into the knot and asked, "What's this about?" The woman blurted out, "My oldest daughter's in drug rehab!" and she proceeded to tell me how one child was acting out the entire family's pain of the parents' recent divorce.

When I find tension in the pectoral (upper chest) muscles that feels emotional, I suspect issues about fatherhood are involved. This can be oneself as father or with any of one's fathers, grand-fathers, male mentors, etc. I find stuck energy relating to one's responsibilities in the back area between the ridges of the shoul-der blades. I find unprocessed resentment in the front knob of the shoulder. [Fig. 6.1]

My point is not to map every emotion that could be stored in your body. Every body is different and what matters most is your experience of your own body. I want to show you how you can discover emotions stuck in *your* body and give you tools to work with them.

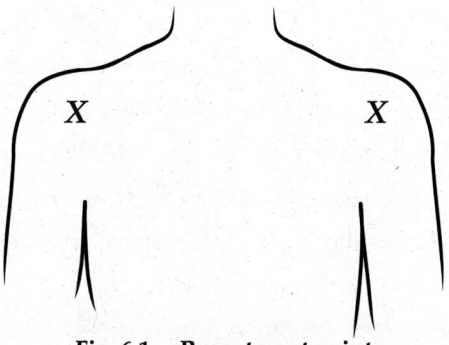

Fig. 6.1   **Resentment points**

Take this idea of resentment in the front of the shoulder joint, for example. A few years back, the front of my shoulder joint on both sides became increasingly sore, the right shoulder more so than the left. I pressed my thumb into that area and breathed deeply and realized I was feeling resentment about my job. I had a talk with myself about it. Yes, there were aspects of the job I didn't enjoy and a couple of people I didn't like working with, but overall, it was a good job, and I appreciated having it. I breathed deeply while allowing myself to feel resentment. After a few minutes of breathing and massaging the stuck spots, the soreness was gone, and I didn't feel negative about my job. I had connected the dots and cleared a layer of stuck emotion. Then, every time I'd feel soreness in those areas, I'd let myself feel the resentment, breathe, and then let the energy move on through.

Then, if I found soreness that felt like it had an emotional charge in that same area, I'd ask my clients while I was pressing there if there was something they were feeling resentful about. They all said yes—some explained, some didn't. I also asked people who were not sore there if they were feeling resentful about anything. The response was consistently "No, I can't think of anything." Every answer I get from a body—mine or another's—helps me understand better.

As you think about your own body and the tension you carry there, you may notice that you carry more tension on your right or left side. The physical answer would be that you use one side more than the other. But this hypothesis doesn't play out. Many right-handed people are far more tense along their left sides. *Mental* (*a.k.a.* masculine, father, yang) energy from thoughts we keep running coalesces on the right side of the body. *Emotional* (*a.k.a.* feminine, mother, yin) energy coalesces on the left side. My resentment had both mental and emotional aspects to it and they showed up on the right and left sides, respectively. Energy from my resentful *thoughts* were accumulating in my right shoulder and my resentful *feelings* accumulated in the left side. I had to allow myself to feel the resentment, let the energy flow through to unblock the left side and release my resentful thoughts to let the energy flow through on the right. Eventually my shoulder was pain-free. If the pain recurs, I know I have some resentment to release and I repeat the process.

Use the following exercise to bring these concepts home in your body. It is designed to get you comfortable with the idea of inquiring into your body for your own answers to what you are feeling. Come back to it any time you want to test out ideas about what emotions are stored in your body or why you might be feeling pain in any given spot.

EXERCISE 6: **Exploring the Issues in *Your* Tissues**

1.   Take a full, slow, belly breath. Now take another.

2.   Rub and poke around in the bony front area of your shoulder joint. If you find a sore spot there, press into it and breathe. Ask yourself if you're feeling resentful about anyone or anything. If you recognize resentment, explore inside yourself to find what it's about. Connecting the thoughts, feelings and physical sensations initiates the healing release. Rub the sore spot and keep breathing fully. If it's still sore, come back later and try this again.

3.   Now ask your body where *it* wants you to explore, and rub or press into that spot as you breathe fully. You probably have an area or two that tightens up on you or gives you pain from time to time. You may already be familiar with a painful area and know what emotions you store there. Start with the obvious spots and probe around to find ones you aren't as familiar with. See if you get any feeling or impression of emotion. Keep breathing into that area and listening for what it's trying to tell you as you touch it.

4.   Continue to do this with any other sore spot you have. Focus inward as you feel around the spot. Press into it or just hold it, and breathe. Allow thoughts or images to arise. Remember when pain has flared up before or times you were especially aware of that area. Let it speak to you. Allow the energy to flow through and out. Breathe.

5. Probe the opposite side of the body. For example, if you immediately went to the right side of your lower back, feel around in the corresponding spot on the left side. Feel if you have more stuck energy or sore spots on one side than the other. Note that.

6. Explore emotional issues with other people. The point is not to pry into others deep wounds or psychoanalyze them. Sometimes it's easier to recognize the emotional issues of others than see your own and you can deepen your understanding as you widen your investigation. For example, if you know someone for whom resentment is an issue, see if they have an especially sore spot on the front of either shoulder. The energetic congestion might be in a slightly different physical location from person to person but it's easy to feel with a little practice. It's fascinating to try out these ideas for yourself and see how other bodies work. No two bodies hold emotion exactly the same way and sometimes contrast can be as enlightening as a similarity.

Even when there's an obvious structural problem a little digging often brings to light an equally obvious emotional component to the problem. I have worked with several women with teen-onset scoliosis, for example, whose spines began to twist out of form as they felt more and more rejected by their fathers. One woman in particular had been her father's "little guy" growing up. Her father had always wanted a son, so he pushed her into sports, and she excelled. As she reached adolescence and her body became womanly, she could no longer compete in baseball and other "boy" sports, and she switched to volleyball and softball. She noticed her father growing more and more distant, more critical and unloving. This change could have come on for many reasons but she interpreted it as her shortcoming in not being the son he'd always wanted. Her thoughts of inadequacy played into her skeleton through feelings of inadequacy and rejection as she could not reconcile the form she had with the form she felt her father wanted her to have. Once she made that connection and made peace with herself as a woman, things began to shift in her body. She retried healing treatments that had not worked previously and new x-rays show her spine to be significantly less crooked now. As the thoughts shifted, the emotional and the physical dimensions shifted as well.

Dr. John Sarno calls the back a "storehouse of emotions" in his book, *Healing Back Pain*[14]. The shoulders carry tremendous loads without much complaint but when the strain becomes too much, tension overflows into the lower back. The lower back seems to have little tolerance for stress and lets us know right away. When people complain of lower back pain, I usually point out the massive tension in their shoulders and upper back and suggest that if they unload tension from the shoulders and neck, the lower back may not need to complain so vehemently.

I notice that issues about *self* such as self-esteem and self-identity coalesce around the solar plexus. I can usually tell a newlywed by the energetic agitation in the back (or front) of

---

14   Sarno, John. *Healing Back Pain*, (Warner Books, 1991)

that area. I've especially noticed tension there in women for whom their new name (changing it or not) is an issue, and in older bachelors getting married for the first time.

If I find lots of tension in the belly—the area where we get "that sinking feeling"—I suspect fear is an issue. People with a lot of issues around fear probably see a gastro-internist or perhaps a homeopathic doctor for what ails their tummies more often than they see a massage therapist. I have consistently found concern for a loved one, such as a brother with cancer or a suicidal mom, in the muscles on the insides of the clavicle bones. In my experience, fear can be a part of any physical problem; it is such a primordial emotion some say it is the root of every negative emotion. If total, unconditional love is at one end of the emotional spectrum, fear is probably at the other end.

As Louise Hay says, the legs seem to relate to issues about forward motion on all levels. I have noticed the calves seem to be extra tight in people who resist going forward with something major in their lives. (I mean deep, chronic tension, not the soreness of a day of over training.) Most of the people I've worked on, myself included, have at least some chronic tension in their calves. It seems to be natural for humans to be somewhat resistant to change and this may be a reflection of that. I have worked on people whose calves were so tight they could hardly walk. A little digging showed massive resistance to moving forward in their lives such as going through with a divorce or quitting a long-held but unhealthy job. The tension inhibits them from moving forward, literally, thereby helping to avoid the feared change.

I once worked on a man with no discernable tension in his calves. He was a man who spent his life moving from one place to another. Despite surpassing skill as a massage therapist he never stayed long enough in one place to establish himself professionally. He continually skipped from one personal relationship to another and, despite his ability to make friends easily, seldom returned to the ones he'd made. In a word, his whole life had to change constantly. When I worked on him, I gave him as much specific pressure in his calves as I could to see if I could reach a painful limit. We couldn't find one. No amount of pressure I could give was too much. He had plenty of limits (places where too much pressure was painful) in other parts of his body, but he seemed to have none in his calves. I took this as the exception that proves the rule.

There is no one area that I would say is "about" sexual trauma. The feelings associated with having our sexual boundaries violated are emotionally and physically complex. Such experiences affect a person on different levels and in different areas at once. The heart area may store the feelings of guilt and betrayal; the belly may store fear; the hips may store feelings of victimization or powerlessness. If I get the intuitive message "sexual trauma" from a body, it's usually when I'm working on the hips. But I almost never mention what I am feeling there unless I also get the feeling of an entrée somewhere else. It is as if the emotions held there are too raw, too gut-level, and I sense that my saying something directly would just shut the person down. I might move to working on another part of the body and see if I am guided to tell one of my stories about someone else with sexual trauma issues.

The woman in the following story had an energetically armored body holding several layers of trauma. Her body had every reason to armor itself. But she had come to a point in her life where her whole being wanted release from her debilitating habit of stuffing down unwanted emotion. The pain she suffered motivated her to stick out the healing, even when it got uncomfortable. I have told her story many times to people on the table who needed a hero to light the way through intense pain and fear and show them how healing might be for them.

The Onion of Incest

Vicky came to me after running the gamut of the medical establishment. An overweight, interior design architect of 46 with the tight-lipped manner of a poker player, she had begun to experience mysterious and sudden pain in her upper back behind her left shoulder blade. The pain was so severe that she would have to go home from work and wait out the "attack." She had seen back specialists, osteopaths, and chiropractors. They ordered x-rays and MRI scans. No one could find a physical problem that would explain her pain. (I say she is lucky that none of these specialists found a physical problem to justify unnecessary surgery.) Finally, a Network® Chiropractor also found that her bones were aligned properly and suggested she go see a massage therapist because maybe the problem wasn't entirely structural. Then, a mutual friend recommended she come see me. She was willing to do whatever it would take to heal her back.

Once she was on my table, she told me that some days she felt fine, working long hours over a drafting table without a problem. Other days, her back would seize up in excruciating pain—sometimes after only twenty minutes of work—and she would have to go home and lie down. Painkillers didn't help. Even tranquilizers could not drug her out of her misery. She didn't see any pattern to what brought on the pain. It was like having an unpredictable migraine in her back.

I could see Vicky was in the midst of a healing crisis. She repeatedly said that she no longer felt comfortable in her overweight body. As she told me about all she had been through, my hands felt her body screaming for help and yet I sensed resistance from her personality. Talking about what was going on was clearly difficult for her. She had the habit of pausing and making a small "hmm" sound right before she said something, as if she had to force the words through a small opening, or as if her will was battling her mind to get the words out. I wanted to bypass the self-censoring that was going on, so when she had finished telling me about all the people she had seen looking for a diagnosis, I pressed on the hot spot I felt in her back and asked, "What's going on in *here*?"

If I had tried to talk with Vicky about her "issues," with her fully clothed, not pushing the "button" at the back of her heart, I imagine she would have said nothing, turned, and fled. (I asked her later and she said she would have.) But there she was, naked under a sheet, wanting to find out why her back was hurting her so much. She had specifically come to me for help in exploring the emotional layers of her pain and she was willing to trust me.

She told that some months before, she had written letters to her family telling them she was no longer willing to carry around the burden of the incest she had experienced as a girl. The pain and shame of her secret, her father's secret, that she suspected the family knew about but was unwilling to discuss, was too much for her psyche and her body to bear any more. I could feel the effort it took to say all of that. I also could feel she was waiting for my reaction. I felt only respect and admiration for her courage—no blame or judgment.

I said, "What I feel here is heartache. That's why it's behind your heart. What do you feel most about what happened with your father?"

"I feel betrayed," she said. My question went directly to the source of the pain and that's where her answer came from.

"Yes, and it's here," I said, pressing again so she could connect the thought, the emotion, and the painful sensation in her body. "Someone else experiencing incest might hold the pain in the stomach if fear was the strongest emotion associated, or in their hips if victimization was the strongest feeling. For you now, the feeling presenting itself is betrayal and it's lodged in your heart area."

As I pressed and rubbed the painful area, she held her breath trying to escape from it. We talked about how she held her breath to block out the pain but by doing so she was actually trapping the pain inside. I coached her to deepen her breathing. Gradually she began to breathe into the pain. Each time she felt the pain and didn't shrivel up and die, she built confidence to go deeper into it the next time it arose.

I continued working down the back of her legs, talking with her to help her understand and integrate what she was feeling. I told her to pay attention when her pain attacks came on and to what she was doing or feeling just prior that might trigger the process. I agreed with the doctors that there was nothing structurally wrong with her back. Nor was her pain "psycho-somatic." She had a very real healing crisis going on, and her body was doing everything it could to help point her attention in the appropriate direction.

Over the next few sessions her energy, openness and ease in her body improved dramatically. I marvel at the courage it took for her to come back to see me each time. Sometimes I would see her again within a few days of a session; other times it would be many weeks before she was ready to dig into and let go of more layers of repressed feelings.

Often she would call me on an evening when she noticed herself mowing down chocolate doughnuts and realized she was trying to stuff down emotions. She readily agreed that overeating and carrying extra weight was her unconscious way of defending herself against pain. She had started to overeat as a girl who didn't want to feel like a sexual object or appear as one to her father or anyone who brought those feelings up for her. It magically worked out that whenever she called me, I could see her right away. My children were very young then and I usually couldn't take last-minute appointments, but an opening always appeared for her right when her pain was up for clearing and easily accessible.

I say her pain was "easily accessible" because I didn't have to dig for it. The process wasn't at all easy for her. Hers was a crisis of mythic proportions as the part of her psyche that wanted a safe status quo battled the part of her that pushed for health and evolution.

At first she feared that revisiting that wound would kill her. I could feel pain and fear wash over her like waves. I felt the emotions washing over me too, but because they were not my issues, it was as if I got sprinkled but not soaked. She would often shudder, or cry, or both. Every time she allowed herself to feel the pain and she didn't shrivel up or explode, she gained the courage to face her emotions the next time they surfaced. She learned to breathe into the physical pain, letting her breath and energy wash the feelings out like long-accumulated sludge. She also learned she didn't have to battle it alone. It was easier for her to go into that dark place with me there to hold her hand, witness and support her. With practice, she became strong enough to face her inner darkness on her own.

Again, forgiveness played a huge role in releasing the pain. She had to forgive herself for being trusting and vulnerable; forgive herself for blaming herself; forgive her father; and forgive her mother and the rest of the family for insisting she keep silent all those years. There were many layers to process.

As the pain got less frightening and the bouts of it less frequent and lasting, she began to understand its value. She learned to see the pain in her back as a signal that she needed to listen to a feeling. At one point she realized that if her back hadn't started hurting, she probably never would have ventured into the repressed emotions as deeply as the physical pain pushed her to do.

Gradually, Vicky realized she didn't have to feel like a victim. If her mother and father behaved in abusive ways, that behavior came from their lack of love, their deficit, not hers. As a child, she didn't have a lot of practical choice. But as an adult, she could reevaluate the patterns to see if the emotional picture she formed as a child still worked for her now. She saw that her behavior (i.e. playing the role of victim, and mistreating herself) came from her lack of love for herself. Abuse was modeled by her parents, but she had the perspective and power now to choose differently. Most importantly, she realized the pain and lack of love didn't have to be her permanent condition.

Vicky's decision to expose her family's secret preceded the heavy pain attacks, but her body was giving her signals that it needed attention long before the pain became overwhelming. Now she understands her body's symptoms are a call for her attention and is pleased they motivate her to listen to them before things get worse. Exploring her deeply-held fears gave her tools to explore any emotion she isn't entirely comfortable with. Feeling her shudder and sweat through the repressed pain of her incest experiences showed both of us how much a person can endure—like the pain of childbirth—and how that's really the only thing to be done.

Together Vicky and I learned that she had an option for dealing with pain and fear besides letting it overwhelm her or shutting it out completely. Instead of letting it build until it blew her house down, she could allow the pain in, give it an audience, and let it flow on out. Not only did she survive, she felt much better for the process.

Over time, she had fewer and fewer painful attacks. She came to see me when she needed a little extra support, but with each visit I could see her self-confidence and strength growing. She began to lose weight and take better care of herself. She made a trip to visit her family and spoke frankly with her mom, dad, and siblings about what had happened. When their response was not as open or loving as she had hoped, she did not take it as a reflection on herself and didn't get defensive. It was as if a huge tangled knot was unraveling and it would take time to work out. She came to see the pain and even the original trauma as a healing lesson, one of life's unexpected gifts. As she did, the energy she had held knotted up in fear and recrimination became available for her to use in exciting new ways. She has recently moved back closer to her family. She has a wonderful new love relationship, is fit and healthy—playing basketball on a team!—and has her own design business where she works the hours that she chooses, pain free.

The issues in our tissues can have many layers. In Vicky's case, the primary area of tension was behind the heart. Her feelings of betrayal by her father presented themselves behind her heart first, and underneath that were deeper feelings of betrayal by her mother. From her point of view, the fact that her mother knew about what was happening and did nothing to stop it or protect her was as painful as what her father did to her physically. She also had associated tension in her upper shoulder area (mother issues), pectoral muscles (father issues), hips (sexual violation), belly (fear) and solar plexus (self-esteem). These surfaced after the initial tension behind her heart began to ease up enough that energy flowed into those other parts enough to communicate clearly.

We can look at these associations from the emotional to the physical as well. Take anger, for example. If we know unexpressed anger is an issue, traditional Chinese medicine would have us look for signs of congested energy in the liver and its meridian, the thumbs (especially the muscular pad and web between the thumb and index finger), jaw, and breasts (in the form of fibrous lumps). The jaw and associated muscles seem to hold tension from the things we don't say, specifically unexpressed feelings of anger, and frustration.

I remember a woman I worked on several times, who had undergone years of massively invasive orthodontia. She also ground her teeth at night. She hated the orthodontia and resented her parents for insisting she have it. She felt it hadn't been necessary. In addition to massaging out the tension I felt in her jaw directly, I felt she needed some trigger to release additional layers of anger and resentment. We discussed rituals to help unbind stuck energetic patterns and I loaned her my copy of *Inner Work*[15] to give her more ideas of how to go about designing her own ritual. She wound up throwing one of her remaining retainers into the sea to symbolize her intention to let go of the pain and anger stuck in her jaw. This is one of those non-logical, right-brain gestures the body *gets*. This is speaking the body's language. It is working the thought backward and out. When I worked on her after her ritual, there was so much less tension it was as if she had a new jaw.

I recall working on a physician who had a knot in his right shoulder. I immediately got the sense that it was about sadness but no thought that I should discuss it with him. I mentioned the "knot" and he insisted, "It's a nerve plexus! A nerve plexus from my tennis playing days twenty-five years ago." My thought was, *Giving it that name (correctly or incorrectly) doesn't seem to have helped you heal it. It's still there, all these years later.* My impression was that there were strong emotions stored in those tissues and that if he wanted to heal the "nerve plexus" he would probably have to look at the possibility that he was blocking out some

---

15   Johnson, Robert, (Harper & Row, San Francisco, 1986)

emotion as well. He was so adamant about denying any emotional component to his pain that I wouldn't be surprised if he eventually developed stronger, un-ignorable physical symptoms as his body-mind pushed him to work on those issues. He clearly wasn't ready to work on them with me at that moment and I didn't push it.

For years I noticed I sometimes started sneezing as I began to put my children to bed. Sneezing was not a new symptom for me but it was remarkable how some nights—but not others—as I sat down to read them a story, I would go into a violent sneezing fit that left me feeling exhausted. As I started watching myself, I noticed I also start sneezing if I had to get up in the middle of the night to deal with a nightmare or a nighttime accident. I scoured my kids' room a few times to make sure there wasn't some pile of dust or mold that was initiating my sneezing fits. Then I noticed I was sneezing at other times of the day when I was frustrated or irritated, and realized there was a psychological component to it. I looked up "sinus problems" in Louise Hay's book and found: "probable cause: irritation to one person, especially someone close." Bingo! That rang true. Some nights I was especially tired and didn't feel like reading bedtime stories or getting up in the night. I began to see that I often sneeze when I'm frustrated or angry with someone I love. Now when I have a violent sneezing fit, I check to see if I'm feeling frustrated or angry about something. Usually, the answer is yes. As I pay attention to my feelings and allow myself to feel them, the sneezing stops.

CHAPTER 7—

Emotion—the Missing Link

Emotion is the body's reaction to thought.

~ Eckhart Tolle

We tend to talk about the "mind-body" connection as if that's all there is to the equation. There's no longer any question that what we think affects our physical body or that our body's condition affects our thoughts. What gets overlooked though, the missing link, is the emotional component in between. We go about our days in a continuous mind-*emotion*-body response loop but mostly without being in our bodies enough to *feel* the emotion. The mind wants to bypass that. *How* mind and body affect each other depends on the emotional spin, the positive or negative *charge*, of the energy exchange. And bringing conscious awareness to that emotional spin is critical for shifting into better health.

Think of thought energy flowing in a lightening-fast response loop that goes from *thought*⇒ *emotion*⇒ *physical response*⇒ *emotion*⇒ *thought*⇒ *emotion*⇒ *physical response* in either a positive or negative direction. Neutral thoughts (no charge, no spin) have little or no effect on the body; more highly charged thoughts have a greater effect. We expand the flow of healthy energy in our bodies by thinking positive thoughts or restrict it by thinking negative thoughts; and breath is the vehicle.

A thought such as "I can do this," or "I love my dog," produces a positive feeling and the body naturally opens the flow of energy and relaxes in response, if very subtly. Breathing opens or stays open. Glee, hope, exuberance, enthusiasm, delight, pleasure, and happiness are all flavors of joy and they link positive thoughts and expanded health. Consciously thinking positive thoughts while breathing fully feels good and opens the flow of life energy through the body. Try it and see if you can feel the opening.

A negative thought such as "I am a victim," or "I'm afraid it won't heal properly," produces an emotion, fear, which results in the body constricting the flow of energy to prepare for a fight, or flight. Anger, sadness, grief, rage, frustration, dread, and angst are all flavors of fear, and they link negative thoughts and declining health. Repeating negative thoughts feels bad and constricts the flow of life energy through the body: breath decreases and health deteriorates.

If you were able to feel an opening while thinking sweet thoughts and breathing, you can play with the closing effect of thinking negative thoughts and restricting breathing. I don't suggest thinking negative thoughts and holding breath to feel a closing unless you open first and open afterward.

While negative thoughts, negative emotions, restricted breathing, and dis-ease have become "normal" and automatic for many of us, there is another option. We can shift a negative spin by bringing conscious awareness to some part of the cycle and diligently choosing a positive alternative. We can intervene in our thoughts by asking, "Is there another way I can respond here? Can I look at it differently and feel better?" When we say "yes" to those questions, when we allow in a better thought, we feel better, our breath opens and energy flows more in our body.

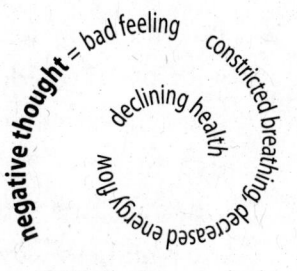

If the negative thought spin is especially strong, we can open energy flow in our body by breathing more fully. Even a few minutes of belly breathing and looking for the positive can really turn around a difficult day. We can support that healthy flow by drinking plenty of clean water, getting good exercise, and eating healthy food. When we do this, we *feel* better. We are treating ourselves with love and that feels *right*. Our energy flows in a positive direction and our thoughts improve.

You can take a few belly breaths and feel your emotions shift. You can smile and feel ease and flow in your body. Try it now. Smile and take a full belly breath. Yes, do it now, even if you don't feel like smiling, smile and breathe deeply. The old adage of "Fake it til you make it" applies here. There's no rush. (If you can't easily take a big belly breath, read Chapter 1 and come back here when you've learned to breathe like you mean it.) I'm taking belly breaths as I type these words and I feel energy flowing down out of my head and through my body. I think I'll get up, drink some water, and stretch.

Ahhhh, that's better! My mind was hogging the energy but when I gave it a chance, my body told me I was thirsty and stiff.

A long history of negative spin from trauma and pain may take more work to reverse as the charge is deeply ingrained. But you know where you're headed if you don't work on this stuff… and you don't have to do it alone! You can get help from someone else to help you spin your energy patterns in a positive direction. That's what psychotherapy aims to do. That's what massage aims to do. Yoga classes, support groups—there are countless ways to intervene in a negative cycle and start your mental-emotional-physical energy moving in a more positive direction. Set your intention and be open to receive help. Greater well-being is well worth the effort.

You probably know someone who has tried to lose weight or quit smoking and—despite tremendous effort and repeated attempts—cannot seem to manage it. Often such a pattern is an indication of deeper psychological and emotional issues that are not addressed by strictly physical solutions. The negative spin is deeply ingrained on several levels. Unconsciously putting on extra weight can be the psyche's way of defending against the pain of abuse, a way to comfort a wounded sense of self, or a way to perpetuate a familiar self-abusive cycle. It doesn't help that our society is so disapproving of overweight people or that so much of the food available to us is full of empty calories that don't nourish us but accumulate as fat.

I believe—and hundreds of my clients have confirmed—that smoking cigarettes is the playing out of a death wish. It may be only one small voice in an otherwise-joyful chorus, but it is the voice that can spoil the symphony and ruin a person's health. Adolescence is a time many people flirt with the idea of their own death. When this natural morbidity combines with peer pressure, the need to rebel, and (often) battered self-esteem, you can see why the majority of people who smoke started during adolescence. And of course, nicotine is addictive. In my experience, what sets apart those who quit smoking relatively easily from those who never quite manage it, however, is the release or persistence of the death wish. This means recognizing the part of the self that wants/wanted to die and why. If a person sees that this desire to die no longer holds true —say for a new mother who now has a strong desire to live—it can be simple to let it go. Others may need to dig a bit deeper. Once the death wish has been addressed and released, the will to live is plenty strong enough to battle the craving for nicotine.

Death Wish

One day I sat down for a quick lunch at the only available seat in a public food court. I started talking with the woman seated across from me and in the course of the conversation she told me she wanted to give her friend a massage for his fiftieth birthday but didn't know a good massage therapist. She was unsure whether he would want it but she felt he needed one. I told her about the work I do. Without missing a beat, she pulled out her purse and said, "You're the one. I'm going to pay you right now. What do you charge? If he doesn't take it, I will."

Two days later I got a call from her friend, Robert, to set up an appointment. He laughed when I told him his friend thought he might not redeem his massage. He replied, "Are you kidding? This is just what I've been needing."

The man I met at the door was a slender 5'10," with an ashen cast to his tanned skin. I intuited cigarettes rather than smelling them directly. We talked about the photographs on my walls. We had some shared acquaintances and interests. With the usual preliminary questions, I asked about injuries and his physical condition. He told me of an old shoulder injury and a bum ankle—nothing remarkable for a man of fifty. I started working on his back. The area behind his lungs felt tight and dry, and congested—the way I feel it in most smokers. He told me that his fiftieth birthday was the next day. I asked, "What does turning fifty mean for you?"

He said, "You know, I've been thinking a lot about that. I've spent the past three years writing the story of my life. I've written it in three books. And what I've learned is that I really don't have any need to keep going."

"Is that why you smoke?"

He pulled his head up out of the face cradle. "How'd you know I smoke?"

"I can feel it in your body. Your back's tight behind your lungs the way a smoker's is." I didn't mention the gray, lackluster quality of his skin. "To me, smoking cigarettes indicates the person has a hidden death wish."

"That's amazing," he said.

"Not really. Maybe sixty years ago people could claim they didn't know cigarettes will kill them, but with all the information we have these days anybody who smokes knows it's deadly. Plus, on some level, you *feel* it. I just worked on a woman last week who was startled to have it put to her that way, but after thinking about it, she said, 'It's true!'."

"No, I mean amazing that you're so accurate about me."

"About your death wish?" I asked.

"Yeah. I've actually quit several times, once for three months. And I feel a whole lot better. Then something pulls me back to it."

"Why do you want to die?"

"Well, I've had a good life. I have no kids, no woman I'm really excited about. I teach a few classes but I'm not really contributing much to anyone. A hundred years ago, fifty years was a respectable life span. I think that's enough for me."

"So that's it. You write your memoirs and you check out?"

"I don't know. Maybe."

"You don't *feel* like someone who wants to die. I don't think you would be here, on this table right now, if you were ready to die. You called right away. You were eager for some healing."

"You have a point," he said. I liked this guy.

"Maybe you just need some new direction, a shift of perspective.

"What matters to you? I mean, what makes your heart pound, what really fires you up?"

"Capturing the moment, the light, just right."

"What else?"

"The feel of a woman's body next to mine."

"Oh, I just felt something, here in your hips." My hands were working on his lower back but as he said that, they felt the energy change in his hips. "Tell me more about that."

"I'm a very sensual person—" he stopped himself short. "But I'm very careful. You know how it is these days. You even look sideways at a woman and you get sued for sexual harassment. I don't even casually touch the shoulders of my female students because of that. I'm very sensitive to this sort of thing."

I felt conflicted energy swirling around in his hips. I checked with my intuition for a moment, then asked, "Were you ever molested as a child?" The impulse was sure and strong.

"No, but funny you should ask. Almost every woman I've ever been with has. Maybe even all of them. Some I didn't ask."

"I feel a lot of conflict in your hip area." I worked down his legs and didn't find anything noteworthy. I asked him to turn over. When he turned over, I picked up each leg in turn and tested its range of motion in the hip socket. His hips were extremely stiff and tight. "Do you dance?" I asked.

"Yeah, I like to dance." This puzzled me. Most people who have hips that tight don't dance. I wouldn't think it would be comfortable. "What about your mother?" I asked. Again, my intuition guided this question.

"What do you mean?"

"Do you know if she was ever molested, raped?"

"She was a Catholic!" he said, indignantly.

I had to laugh at that one. "What?! So Catholics never get molested?"

"Well, yeah. I mean. . . Well, I don't know. That's not something we would ever talk about."

"There's something here, in your hips, about your mother

and sexuality." An insight was forming in my mind. "Often I feel a certain blocked energy in a woman's hips if she's been sexually violated. But I'm realizing that what I'm feeling may well be that your mother was violated. And her feelings of fear and anger got transferred to you. What do you think?" As I said this, goosebumps bloomed up my arms and legs—my personal indicator of truth.

I could feel energy starting to move in Robert's body. "I'm a very sexual person. But I've never been able to. . . I mean, I've always felt restrained, like I can't express the full extent of it. It would be a lot."

"It would make sense to me if she had been violated, that she would unconsciously shut down her son's sexuality. Either to make sure her son wouldn't do that to anyone else or in retaliation for what had been done to her. I doubt she would have consciously known she was doing it." I kept getting waves of goosebumps, which told me I was on target. Then I got the impression of red.

"I'm getting an image of you wearing red." Again, a question popped into my head "Did you ever play dress up?"

"Yeah, I have two older sisters. They used to dress me up sometimes. I used to love the feel of women's clothes on my skin. The silky textures felt so good to me."

"Something about when you were five years old."

"Oh my God!" He said suddenly. If he had been hooked up to an oscilloscope, the lines would have been jumping. "I used to have this red cowboy shirt that I wore all the time. I loved that red cowboy shirt. I was such a free little kid. I have a picture of myself sitting with my grandmother. My mom's in the picture, or maybe she took it. The negative is back in Connecticut. I've been wanting to reprint it."

I rested my hands lightly on the sides of his hips through the towel, listening carefully and ready to nudge it if the flow got stuck. "Tell me more about that photo."

"I'm wearing my red cowboy shirt in the photo."

"What do you feel?"

"I want to get away from them." He paused. "That's the moment! That was when my spontaneity evaporated."

"What else?" I asked.

He was feeling the energy held in his body. "Fear. I feel fear."

"What about your grandmother?" I asked.

"She's part of it too. The fear."

"Is the fear theirs or yours?"

"Both." I saw tears in the corners of his closed eyes. "I was such a free little kid," he lamented. "That was the moment it got shut down."

"Maybe that's when you got the message that to please them, to be a male in their family, you had to put a lid on your own sexuality. Because of their fear. You may come from a line of abused women who needed to shut down your sexuality."

"Yeah."

"Could you go back and have a talk with that free little kid you were? Maybe find something red to put on and reconnect to that sensual, alive little boy. That's where you left your joy. I bet once you find him again, he'll be able to tell you what you have to live for, what you have still to do with this life you have."

"Yeah, maybe that's it. It's like everything got frozen the moment that photo was taken."

"How about a ritual? I have this great book I can lend you.

(I was thinking of *Inner Work* by Robert Johnson[16].) It shows you how to unblock the stuck energy from a moment like that. Going through the motions, physically, can unlock the energy that's stuck in your body." I paused, listening. "Something about putting your arms through red sleeves." I was working on his arms now. "Does that red cowboy shirt still exist?"

"No. My mother threw it away. She was . . . she was a good woman but . . . she was pretty shut down herself."

"What about a silky red negligée? I know a great costume store. I bet you could find something playful there that would help you reconnect to that spontaneous little boy you were. Could you do that?"

"Yeah, maybe. I have to reprint that photo. I was thinking of taking a trip back there anyway." He was clearly on his own inner roll.

"What do you think five-year-old Robert would think about your smoking?"

"He'd think I was out of my mind!"

"He loves life, doesn't he?"

"Yeah he does!"

"Do you think you could stop smoking? Embrace life?"

He faltered. "I don't know."

"Maybe if you had little Robert's help?"

"Yeah, I think so."

I loaned Robert my copy of *Inner Work* and encouraged him to play around with dressing up in something red. I felt sure I would see him again.

Several months later, I ran into Robert at the beach. I couldn't

---

16   Johnson, Robert. *Inner Work* (Harper & Row, 1986)

place him at first. He had just come out of the water and something about him had changed significantly. He was with a good-looking woman about his age. And he looked wonderful. He told me that he is working on three completely different books and doing great.

"You're loving life?" I asked pointedly.

He said, "Yeah, I am."

The woman bent down to brush sand off her legs. I mimed smoking a cigarette and raised my eyebrows to ask if he was still smoking. He grinned and shook his head emphatically, no.

"I'm so glad!" I said. "That's great news."

In Robert's case, the thoughts and emotions had been buried for decades but they were readily accessible. Once he was open and his energy was flowing, it was simply a matter of making connections between the negative messages from his childhood and his thoughts, feelings, and physical responses to them. Making the connections initiated healing on many levels for him.

Most of us can readily recall harsh trauma that has happened to us—sometimes in horrifying detail. As we replay those tapes, we etch those negative feelings deeper in our psyches and in our bodies. We fall into the groove of depression or dis-ease more easily if that's what we focus on. But in the same way, we can give our attention to positive experiences, thoughts and feelings and have those show up more often.

Giving more energy to positive thoughts that produce positive feelings and ease and space in the body. You can start a collection of sweet memories and delicious moments that you can access to feel better in times of stress or upset. They can be like beautiful pebbles you carry in your pocket and finger when you need comfort or solace. They can be like a file of jokes on your computer you open when you need a laugh.

I started my collection of what I now call "Click-and-Save moments" many years ago. I was in college, at a chamber concert with a dear buddy I had known since eighth grade. The concert was held in a huge stone chapel and part of the audience got to sit on the stage with the musicians. The music was heavenly, slow and sensual—especially inspired in that huge, hallowed space. I felt safe and warm, completely centered and content, and I realized that this was a moment I would want to remember my whole life. So I took note of all the details I could.

I noticed the cool, mossy-smell of the stone walls, the gorgeous colored light filtering in through the stained-glass windows, and the way the sounds danced off the high walls and ceiling. I looked over at my friend, Phil, and felt love for him and all the things we had gone through together. I remember feeling open and energetic in my body and connected to the glory that humans express through the arts. It was a moment of pure bliss. To this day, I can close my eyes, transport myself back into that stone chapel, smell the mossy coolness, and feel that open-hearted bliss. When I do, my breathing immediately deepens and I get a sweet feeling of well-being. All the vivid sensory details I noticed helped anchor that moment deep in my body.

You can start a collection of such moments and take them out when you need a little lift, when you want to feel better, and for

practice spinning your thoughts and feelings in a positive direction. You may already have moments like this in your memory
that you can build on. Any moment of pure joy—especially
if you clearly remember what it felt like in your body—is a
moment to consciously add to your "file."

EXERCISE 7: The Click-and-Save Exercise

1.   Call up moments in your life where you felt healthy and
alive and at peace with yourself and the world. A triumphant
moment is an easy place to start. Recall a time you felt joy in
your body, such as riding a bike for the first time, standing
on a winner's podium, or getting a congratulatory hug from
a loved-one. Once you find such moments, your collection is
already started. Take that good-feeling moment and flesh it
out with all the sensory details you can. Recall the sounds
you heard, the colors around you, how you felt in your body.
If you can't remember specific smells or sounds, imagine
them to give depth and texture to the memory file. For this
process, the open, joyful feeling is more important than
historical accuracy. The point is to expand and practice your
feelings of well-being.

2.   Notice your breathing and feel inside your body.
When you feel good, your breathing deepens. Aches and
pains diminish as the energy flows more. Feel around in
your body to experience how those good feelings translate
in your joints and muscles. Maybe your eyesight gets a
bit clearer. Notice the smells of your surroundings. Are
they outdoor smells? human smells? city smells? Notice

the light, the sounds. What are you wearing? Who else is there? Get as detailed as you can. This is important practice being in the here and now and *in your body*.

3. From now on, watch for times you feel fabulous, relaxed, or content in your skin. When you identify a click-and-save moment, take note of all the physical sensations in your body and the sensory details of your environment. The details you notice help deepen and enrich the memory and give it more handles, more heft. This makes the memory file easier to find. Consciously save those good-feeling memories to an experiential file in your mind. You can revisit those expanded feelings any time you want to feel better.

4. Sometimes the simple moments are the sweetest— like sitting in the sun stroking your beloved pet, kissing your baby goodnight, or waking up next to your beloved. A Click-and-Save moment can be any time that it feels especially good to be alive.

5. Continue to look for moments of triumph, love and success to click and save—like when you celebrate the completion of a challenging project at work; when you give a special present to someone; or when your child first learns to pump on a swing. Do this any time you feel strong, healthy, or in sync with life. You can "click on" those good-feeling thoughts to change your mood any time you feel bad—in the same way you use a TV remote control or the mouse on a computer to switch to a better program.

6. Build your collection of click-and-save moments. At a superb concert, walking your beloved dog, laughing with your children—any time you feel fully alive and great— notice your breathing, the smells, the light, the feelings in your body. Notice the expanded circulation, the warmth of connection, a feeling of having more space in your body. You can carry those feelings like smooth pebbles in your pocket and you can get one out and enjoy the feel of them when you need comfort. Revisit them often. The more your body practices the expanded circulation, full breathing, and contentment of such moments, the more you will attract and live more feelings of well-being.

☯

The 1960s and '70s saw a explosion of discussion about our emotions and their role in our overall health. We began to understand how external events affect our thoughts, our thoughts become our emotions, and they, in turn, motivate our behavior. People flocked to analysts' couches looking to talk out the pain of their emotional wounds. But that didn't always work. Therapy can help people develop a clear, intellectual picture of their problematic emotions without ever actually feeling them. A person with a strong mind can understand and then talk circles around his or her emotional wounds for years in psychotherapy. I did it myself to the point where I saw no way past my own mental defenses. The only way past my mind was with a holistic—intuitive, psychological *and* physical—approach. I used intuitive bodywork to access the energy stored *in my body* and

I DIDN'T HAVE TIME TO "FEEL" ANYTHING. I WAS JUST FROZEN
IN THE MIDDLE OF THE ROAD, LIKE, LIKE I DON'T KNOW WHAT

intuitive, playful counseling to access my emotions. By connecting those aspects of myself, I bypassed my mental defenses and I was able to begin healing the wounds they protected. In effect, I was spinning the thought loop in the positive direction. The combination of conscious intention and integrated approach made all the difference.

Releasing deep emotional wounds doesn't have to be a long, grueling process. It can be simple and fast. In the following story you will see what happens when a brave young woman neatly lays down her mental defenses instead of trying to beat her way past them. Bringing awareness to the unconscious patterns *in her body* shifted her whole feeling about herself.

Going Large

Tanita reminded me of myself at the age of twenty-five. She took on the world with her strong mind and had an answer for everything. She came for her first-ever massage at a crossroads in her life, specifically ready for some healing to happen. She said her head hurt her most of the time and she had massive neck and shoulder tension. She had come to a standstill in her career, intimate relationships, and health. She had lost touch with her body, felt little or no emotion, and spent all of her time in her head. She desperately needed to get out of her mind and re-establish her connection with herself. She was ready for a change, ready to heal, but she wasn't sure how it would happen. We got right to work.

I asked her several times, "How does this feel?" as I pressed on this knot, or worked that muscle. She didn't know what to answer. It was as if her body was speaking a language she didn't understand anymore. I spent much of the session teaching her to breathe deeply and pay attention to the sensations in the tense, emotion-charged parts of her body. I worked extra-long on the tension in her neck, which initially felt like immovable concrete. She was determined to get the most out of her massage and she bravely focused on her resistance and breathed into it when it would have been easier not to. She was listening intently to everything I was saying but I had no idea what effect it would all have. We finished the session and I thought that was the last I'd see of her.

Two days later, she booked another session with me, this time for two hours. When I saw her the second time, I hardly recognized her. She looked bigger and taller, as if she took up more space. The first time I had met her, her energy must have been pulled in. Now she not only filled out her body with energy but also filled even the space beyond her body with it. She had gone large with herself. She said that after our last session she had taken a long walk along the beach and realized her whole perspective had changed. She loved what had happened and, even though she was a little afraid, she wanted more of it, more healing. I told her I would take her as far as we could go together. With two hours ahead of us and her fierce resolve to heal, we were both ready for something big to happen. (I'll report our exchange in interview format to give you the sense of its focused intensity.)

I said a prayer asking for guidance. Both of us went directly into the focused, trance-like state that precedes and facilitates healing, with intuition invited and engaged. Her right shoulder seemed tightest. My intuition said, *over controlling due to fear*.

Denise: "What are you afraid of?"

Tanita: Everything.

D: You're carrying a big burden. What is it?

T: Everybody's pain. It hurts.

D: Why do you carry it?

T: I want to protect them.

D: You aren't helping them by carrying their burdens. When they go to work on their own stuff, it isn't there. You've got it. [I get the idea to do the following:] Okay, picture your mother. In your mind's eye stand her up in front of you right here. Can you see her? [After a moment, she nods.]

Give her back her pain. [Nothing happens.] Try saying, "Mom, I give you back your pain."

T: Mom, I give you back your pain. [Shudders, starts crying]

D: Now forgive her.

T: [Nods. Big sigh.]

D: Forgive yourself.

T: [Nod, big sigh.]

D: Now your father. What's his name?

T: Paul. No. Not Paul, Don. [I presume one is her biological father and the other one did the *fathering*.]

D: Put Don in front of you. You now, as an adult, in your power. Give him back his pain. Forgive him. Forgive yourself.

T: [Shudders, cries.]

D: Now Paul.

T: [Shudders, cries.]

D: Who else?

T: My sister.

D: [I feel her shift and tighten.] What do you feel?

T: It hurts so much.

D: You love her.

T: Yes.

D: What's her name?

T: Dara.

D: Tell her you love her and give her back her pain.

T: It hurts. [To sister] I give you back your pain. I give you back your loneliness.

D: How do you feel?

T: Better.

D: Forgive her.

T: [Nods.]

D: Forgive yourself.

We continued this process with several other significant people in her life, especially men who had mistreated her or who hadn't honored her. Each time her shoulder relaxed a little. She cried plenty. It sounds fast and mechanical the way I wrote it, but it is often like that at the eye of the storm: no drama, just intense and real. At one point, she got up from the table to blow her nose and go to the bathroom. I finished massaging her body but felt no other places of blockage. That doesn't mean she didn't have other areas to work on in the future, just that her body had released what it was ready to release at the time and nothing more was presenting itself.

We talked about how it doesn't help her loved ones for her to carry their burdens for them. She had her arms so full of everyone else's burdens, she couldn't carry anything else —certainly not her own burdens or her own joy.

As she got up and dressed, she seemed relieved—empty, and also fuller. She was breathing deeply.

"You've changed my life," she said. "I want to do for other people what you've done for me." She gave me a big hug. She seemed so much bigger.

"Bravo!" I said. "Own it for yourself, then pass it on. That's what it's all about."

Bringing breath back into her body and re-opening her neck as a conduit for energy to communicate between her body and her mind started Tanita's own personal renaissance. Her strong intention to heal carried her smoothly through the rough spots. The deeper lesson came through loud and clear: carrying someone else's burdens doesn't truly serve them. We both got it.

If that story rings a chord with you, simply recognizing that you have repressed emotional energy in your body might be an important first step. Ask yourself, "Is there anything I don't allow myself to feel?" and "Am I carrying thoughts, emotions, or projections from others that aren't really mine?" Feeling for emotions stored in your body and consciously exploring where they came from can shed light on unconscious beliefs that may not serve you anymore.

It's common for people to allow themselves to feel certain emotions but not others. I know people whose religious upbringing conditioned them to be more comfortable feeling guilt than free-flowing pleasure. There are people who can rage but not cry, or cry but not laugh. It's as if the holes on their emotional flute get clogged and certain notes can no longer sound. It can get to the point that no matter what they try to express, only one sound (emotion) gets played out.

I know men who can only express anger. Deep inside, they might feel vulnerable or sad but the feeling gets immediately rerouted and then sounds off as a blast of anger. My dad is such a man. When we spilled milk at the dinner table, he sounded furious. When he was scared because he had to go to the hospital, he sounded angry. Even when his mom died, his grief came out looking and sounding like anger, the one emotion he was comfortable expressing. There are so many emotional notes to play in a life. I don't know if my dad realizes what he's missing.

The unconscious thought, *"I can't allow myself to feel sadness—or jealousy, or anger,"* may have persisted for decades but the thought has long outlived its use as a protective defense. Even if it's a new process for you, you can find and revisit those places in your body where you've "dumped" unwelcome emotion and then locked it in by cutting off the breath/energy. A brave breath or two consciously directed into the stuck spot in your body can work wonders to start the process. The work is to look at where your old patterns aren't serving you and step outside your habit enough to see a different possibility—play a different note, if you will. Sometimes giving yourself a few loving breaths is all it takes to unlock decades of frozen emotion.

Fears you had as a child may seem silly from an adult perspective, but they may still have you in their grip. You didn't consciously realize that holding your breath held in your fears but it worked to keep you "safe" from them at the time. With a little practice and attention you can now recognize that your emotions (your physical reactions to thoughts) are governed by what you do with your thoughts and breath. Event *A* doesn't always have to produce emotion *B*. It's as if an event is black and white until the thoughts paint the emotions into your body with their infinite variation of color. You can change the thought that determines what emotion (and physical reaction) gets associated with that event at any time. You can spin the cycle in a positive direction with intention and breath.

For example, imagine that your boss says to you, "You're fired." The external event is indisputable. But how you react emotionally depends entirely on your *thoughts* about that event. If you love your job and feel secure in your position, getting fired would feel like a sudden punch in the gut, a betrayal. Your body will constrict. On the other hand, if you hate your job and secretly (or openly) want to get out of it, getting fired may feel great, a welcomed relief, like being released from jail. Your body will release. The fact of the firing remains neutral but the effect of it depends entirely on your thoughts, which determine your physical and emotional reaction to it.

If you initially react to that news with fear, you can choose –in that moment of awareness—not to spin further into it. You can take a breath and tell yourself you have options. You can start looking for ways that news might be welcome. Every situation has some light if you can step back far enough from it. If you keep breathing and staying centered, you will be able to see the light when it shows up. You can play with your thoughts about anything and choose a better-feeling spin. The old adage about seeing the cup half full instead of half empty has merit if you actually shift your way of looking at a situation. The situation doesn't shift, you do. You feel better.

How about a belly breath right now? Just because you're alive and you deserve it!

☯

CHAPTER 8

Funny You Should Say That— Intuition

Intuition is the supra-logic that cuts out all the routine processes of thought and leaps straight from the problem to the answer.

~ Robert Graves

The *New Oxford American Dictionary*[17] defines *intuition* as follows: "Intuition: *the ability to understand something immediately, without the need for conscious reasoning.*" It is a *knowing* without *thinking*.

Intuition is your conduit into the vast world beyond your human senses, your conduit to *Spirit*. It is the link between your rational mind and the divine, which gives you access to information and insights you might never get any other way. You might say intuition 'senses' the non-physical the way your eyesight senses the visual world. It is definitely non-rational and doesn't lend itself to words or quantification. The linear, rational mind mistrusts an intuitive approach but that doesn't

---

17   *The New Oxford American Dictionary*, 2nd Ed., (Oxford University Press, 2005)

mean it isn't a valid way to access information.

Everybody has intuitive powers. You certainly do. They may have been beaten down by life or suppressed by people around you, but make no mistake, they are there. If you have ever thought to yourself, "I *knew* he was going to say that," or "I was just thinking of her," when you meet someone on the street, that was your intuition giving you information you couldn't *know* rationally.

Culturally, we are skittish about openly discussing intuitive healing because it is not "scientific." Skeptics want verifiable proof. Ever since the Age of Reason, we have been required to fit our knowledge and experience into tidy, replicable boxes. It's not "real" if it's not scientifically verifiable, so the scientific line goes. But so much of our experience doesn't fit into tidy boxes. We've all had miraculous moments of awe and insight, ideas that came "out of nowhere." We probably can't reproduce them but that doesn't mean they didn't happen. Science still doesn't have appropriate tools to quantify and verify intuitive insight. But that doesn't mean it doesn't exist. In cultures that maintain a strong link to the natural world, the shaman, medicine woman, or spirit healer is still and always has been a respected part of daily life.

Intuition is the divine speaking to and through us. Whether we call it God, Spirit, our higher self, the superconscious, or life force, intuition is that larger Being made re-cognizable to us. It is becoming in*spir*ed, full of life's breath, infused with spirit. This is not blasphemy. It's not "hocus-pocus" or "voodoo" (although I suppose voodoo could be intuitive). WE can all connect up or tap into the divine for guidance and inspiration about anything we do. Artists tap in for creative inspiration.

I KNEW HE WAS GOING TO SAY THAT

Monks sit in silence as a vehicle to connect up. One of our greatest scientists, Albert Einstein, said, "There is no logical way to the discovery of these elemental laws. There is only the way of intuition, which is helped by a feeling for the order lying behind the appearance." The process is precious, and it happens all the time. What distinguishes anything that is intuitively inspired is that it somehow transcends the ordinary. There's a creative power there, an energetic spark, more love, or more light.

Children are naturally intuitive. As children, we believed in beings and places that we can't see with our physical eyes. We knew there were wonder-ful things grown-ups didn't see anymore. We had natural faith. But the way our culture dishonored the numinous broke down our natural confidence in the "magical" world and we settled for the mundane.

Many of us were told about Santa Claus and came to love and believe in a red-suited man at the North Pole who delivers presents all over the world with a magical sleigh and reindeer. Then later we were told that Santa does not exist—that it's all just a myth, a made-up story. If our authority figures teach us to believe in something we cannot see and then those same authorities tear it down as "the stuff of childhood", we become skeptical about the reality of all things we cannot see or prove and want to put away "childish" things in order to "grow up."

I remember how outraged my daughter was when she felt her parents had lied to her about Santa. One day the kids at school called her a baby for still believing in Santa. She came home demanding, "Do you wrap the presents?" She badgered me all evening, pulling her little brother into the action. Finally I couldn't dodge the questions any longer. So I said, "When you ask for a truthful answer, I will always give you one to the best of my ability. Are you *sure* you want to know?" She replied, "Yes, I want to know." So I finally said, "Yes, we wrap the presents." This brought a triumphant "Aha!" from her and tears from my son, who didn't want to hear that answer. Then my daughter asked about the Easter Bunny and by the time the Tooth Fairy came up, she, too, was in tears. It was as if her magical vision and her trust in things unseen were destroyed with one blow. No matter how much I talked about the spirit of giving or the magic of the unseen, she felt betrayed.

Whether our intuition has been gently discouraged or thoroughly stomped on, we can give ourselves permission to expand our intuitive ability and practice seeing evidence of it in play—around and in us, all the time.

Like with any ability or sense, some are more strongly intuitive than others. I notice that people who have gone through intense trauma at an early age, or grow up in unstable households, often develop stronger intuition to help them navigate difficulty—the way a blind person may develop stronger hearing to compensate.

Great healers of all types use their intuition more than they usually talk about. I heard the great Hawaiian healer, Kalua, give an intuitive breakdown of his healing work as 40 percent faith (inviting Spirit), 40 percent intention (directed thought), and 20 percent skill (practiced doing). Though we have no way to definitively measure such things, this feels *true* to me. In this context I consider faith an invitation or opening to the divine, setting the stage, asking for help and guidance. Intention is the thought that directs the action, the switch that allows the juice to flow. The intention of the healer to be of service in a healing way opens the door for miraculous possibilities. The intention of the client to receive the healing energy completes the circuit, gives it a place to go. The knowledge and experience of the healer —her skill—directs the details of what takes place.

When conditions are right and the healing energy connects up, I feel like a lightening rod grounding healing energy into a person's body, catalyzing the union of energy and intention to effect healing. In practice, intuition becomes the creative connection. In almost every massage I give, I hear some version of the phrase, "It's funny you should say that." This is because when I'm intuitively tuning in to a person or a situation, I am reading thoughts and emotions I intuit there. I sift through the information I pick up from someone and, because I naturally tune into underlying emotion, I tend to feel (intuit, connect into) thoughts that have especially strong emotional charges to them. You could say that I feel the physical manifestation of the thought. This is coincidence. (Read that word as co-incidence. It is not an accident, but two things happening at the same time.) And it happens through intuition.

You and I can marshal our faith, intention and skill to heal. We are all healers. We heal ourselves, and we can facilitate the healing of others. The healing gift, like the gift of musical ability or any other talent, must be honored, developed and practiced.

An energetic release can range from dramatic, to subtle. Crying, shaking, a sound that erupts from your throat—those are dramatic releases. And usually, because a lot of energy gets moved through, you feel a lot better afterward. You can have a more subtle release that's hard to point to or put into words but is no less *true*. You feel lighter and less cramped afterward. It might feel like there's more space inside your head or body, that you feel more open or less heavy.

The stories in this chapter illustrate (my) intuition in action, giving me information I wouldn't get otherwise. Often with information I receive intuitively, I don't know in the moment how it is important or how I am to use it. In the case of "My Mother's Death", my mother is still alive so I don't know if the information I got will wind up being "accurate," or not. I am in absolutely no rush to find out.

Reports of My Mom's Death are Greatly Exaggerated

This little story is about one of the most precious gifts I have ever received. As I mentioned, my mother's body was my original proving ground. I learned to trust the impressions I received from her body during all that massage I gave her as I grew up. Her body was always so open to me and my mom was so appreciative, that she made tuning in easy and rewarding. My hands are now so attuned to her body that I don't even have to touch her body to know what's going on there.

Several years ago, my mother came to visit me on Maui. She was 64 at the time. We set up my table for a massage, as was our custom. As I was working away, nothing in particular presented itself until I came to her belly. My hands stopped to listen. I felt death —her death —in her abdomen. As I looked up and met my mother's eyes I knew she was feeling the same thing. She sat up and we grabbed each other. I asked, "Do you feel that?" She nodded. We hugged each other in grief and joy, tears streaming down our faces.

"This is our goodbye."

"I think so," she replied.

"Mom, you've been the greatest mother. I'm so lucky I got to grow up with you. Thank you." We didn't need words. I knew she felt my love.

"I'm the lucky one, Denise. You've added so much to my life. My precious girl." I felt her love and I know she felt mine.

"I don't think I'm going to be there when you die."

"I don't think so either," she said.

"But it's not going to be any time soon!" I blubbered.

"I hope not. But it's OK." She seemed so peaceful.

"I know it is. You've had a good life. You've done a lot. You got to see your granddaughter be born." I paused, pulling back and searching her eyes. "But you have to go to Paris! And my children! It's not going to be that long, you know. You can't die before you see my kids, or *Paris*!" Going to France had always been a dream of hers. She had learned French in school but had never even owned a passport. "And you're not sixty-eight! You promised me you'd make it to sixty-eight." My mom had gone through an extremely depressed period several years earlier and when I feared she had lost the will to live, I made her promise me she would live at least to age sixty-eight. My mom absolutely believes one must keep promises to children.

"I think I'll make it that far," She said. "But we both *know*, don't we. Don't let them drag it out. I don't want that." She has always hated the idea of extended life support if one is vegetative.

I shook my head and buried it in her soft shoulder. "I love you so much, Mom." I looked at her again. "Let's communicate, after, I mean. Try to contact me and I'll listen, OK?"

"I'm sure you'll hear me. I'm not worried about that."

"Me neither, I'm not worried. I'm glad we've had a chance to say goodbye. Even if you live another thirty years, we'll have had closure."

"I hope not thirty years, that's too much," she laughed.

"I'm grateful for whatever I get."

About a year after that, my mother went to Paris, by herself, with a shiny new passport. She has since seen the births of five grandchildren, two of them mine. It's now more than seventeen years after that moment. She has diabetes and heart problems that have seen her in and out of the hospital. A few years ago, the threat of insulin shots helped her get serious about watching her diet. She has since lost eighty pounds. At age 77, she made her last trip to Maui and assembled her daughters and grand-children around her. The bottom line is that she still wants to be here and she is. When she decides otherwise, I don't have to worry about getting there in time to say goodbye. We've already said it.

It is no wonder that bodyworkers often become adept at sensing subtle physical messages. Their work gives them ample opportunity to use their intuition to make sense of the information they pick up from the various bodies they work with. I've had dozens of conversations with massage therapists who initially approached massage from a strictly anatomical, physical, and scientific perspective. With attention and practice, they couldn't help but become adept at "reading" clients on non-physical levels as well. I suppose it's similar to the musical process. Through practicing scales and songs, you also gain an understanding of the wider and subtler rela-tionships among notes, instrumental voices and harmonies. Practice and attention helps us tune in to higher and finer levels of experience even beyond our ability to verbalize it. And there are always virtuosi.

One of the aspects of my intuition I enjoy the most is the feeling of connection I get when I've touched the right point. It feels like plugging into an electrical current. I don't always find the right point —it may not be presenting itself to be found or I might be "off" that day —but when I do connect, I am sure. When I open up my intuition to do healing work, I feel loving and warm and clear and the thoughts and impulses seem to come from somewhere other than my mind. Time stops; and I feel connected up and out of my own personality. The information I get happens to be about physical and emotional matters, but that's only one way to be intuitive. Other bodyworkers may use their intuition to guide them where to work in the body without any particular reference to emotions. Medical intuitives perceive diagnostic information—sometimes including the reason for an illness and how it started. The best healers I know are intuitive, this includes MDs. When you are able to bring a strong intuitive insight to the knowledge and experience you already have, your work is bound to be more effective.

The following story is about a question I had that was answered intuitively. As you will see, the insight I got helped me understand a pattern I'd encountered but didn't fully understand. With this experience, I felt I had been handed an important piece of a puzzle I'd been working on.

Deep Roots of Tension

There was a period a few years back when I found myself working almost exclusively on African-Americans. I noticed a consistent pattern of deeply entrenched holding that I couldn't find a way to soften. The muscles in their bodies were more consistently, thoroughly and differently armored than in their Caucasian or Asian counterparts I'd worked on. The pattern reminded me of the defensive energetic tension pattern I often feel in the bodies of policemen. That tension is more emotional than mental and it is very difficult to penetrate. This tension pattern I found in these variously-hued brown bodies was more emotional than mental but deeper and more visceral—like armor worn under the skin as opposed to outside it. I figured it had to do with the discrimination and oppression African-Americans often face in our culture, but some of the people I worked on had led prosperous and privileged lives. There was one man in particular I really wanted to work with further, because I felt enough of an opening in him that I thought I could both help him release the tension pattern and learn more about it myself. But he had come to me on his vacation and I only worked on him once.

One day a few weeks later, I had given several massages but I had energy for one last treatment to round out my workday and I energetically called for one more. —I put out my intention. At the last moment when I was just about to pack up, I saw a woman get up from her lounge chair by the pool and walk over to me. She was roughly 50, sinewy and slender, with a tight cap of salt-and-pepper curls, and beautiful milk-chocolate skin. She told me her name, that she wanted a full-body massage, and lay down on the massage table without another word. I didn't know what would happen but I was ready for something out of the ordinary—because I'd called for it and I could feel an extra electricity.

As I massaged her muscles, images began to parade across my mind's eye. First, of a young black woman in a rough white dress sweeping a stoop, then of her being taken to a shed and raped by a white man. I saw images of children being taken from their mothers to be sold; another white man violating a black girl. I saw men, women, and children being whipped. I saw a family sitting around a fire, mourning a stillborn baby. I saw hard, physical labor and stoic bearing up through pain and anguish. I watched as a white man led away a woman's horse and cow and felt rage and helplessness settle deeper into her body. I intuited the message, *"You want to know why our bodies are so hard? You want to know the pattern we carry? Here it is."*

It was like watching a movie. I thought of Arthur Haley's *Roots* and of Lalita Tademy's *Cane River,* but the scenes playing on my mind's screen were not from any book I had ever read or any movie I had seen. The faces and details were different. The images continued. I saw scenes of hardship where the person's only recourse was to swallow the rage and frustration and sadness and carry on, year after year, generation after generation. Not that this woman had experienced all those hardships herself but they were part of her energetic blueprint. The energetic holding pattern got passed down along with the stories, the strength, and the determination to survive.

The images were almost black and white in that they were not heavily colored with emotional charge. The woman I massaged did not have much fat or muscle tissue. I wondered if her body had always been that way or whether she had consciously worked through the issues of her heritage and come to this point of relative objectivity by releasing the energy that would have made her tissues bulkier and the images more colored with emotional charge.

The woman never said anything during the massage except to nod when I asked if the pressure was right. I have no idea whether she had any idea about the images her body projected to me. When we were finished she thanked me for the massage and tipped me well.

It took me a while to digest that experience. Each of us carries the legacy of our ancestors to some degree. I had seen a vivid intuitive tableau demonstrate that each of us carries the *emotional* blueprint our forebears as well as a physical one. The more we become conscious of what we carry, the better we can choose whether it is something that serves and strengthens us or whether it is something to bless and release.

In the following story, intuition not only guided me to see the bigger picture of what was going on with the woman on my table, it guided me not to make an issue of it. We all need a little reassurance now and then and all I had to do was give some to her.

Infertility!

I remember Susan as a pretty, petite blond who arrived at my beachside massage table with her husband for side by side massages. I watched the obviously loving young couple as they negotiated who would go on which table and wondered at the tension that was also evident between them. Within a minute or two, she told me she didn't have any injuries, lay down on my table, and untied her bathing suit top. I breathed and tuned in.

Her breathing was almost imperceptible as I rocked her hips. Twice I asked her to take a deeper breath but there was no change. I put my hands on her shoulders and felt massive tension. "Oh!" I said.

"I know, I'm tight," she said.

Then I touched the area in back of her heart and my hand jumped up as if shocked by electricity. I pressed into what felt like the eye of a hurricane and said, "Wow, what's this about?"

The word "Infertility!" exploded out of her mouth, catching me by surprise. Usually I have a little more time to learn how to navigate a discussion that intimate with someone. But she launched right into the story of her struggles to get pregnant.

Susan and her husband had been married for three years and after two years of trying to get pregnant on their own, they had spent the past year trying every possible intervention for her to get pregnant. She had undergone endless tests, various surgeries, and different kinds of hormone therapy. She talked about meticulously taking her temperature and timing their intercourse. She said sex had long since become a tense chore and the strain was threatening their marriage. Her husband had insisted they come to Hawaii to relax and take a break from trying. She would do anything it took. She had heard Hawaii is a fertile place and was determined to try all the more.

"Do you want a boy or a girl?" I asked, trying to peek beyond the obsessive rigidity.

"Either one," she replied. "I just want to get pregnant." That was pretty clear.

"Why?"

"Because I want a baby!" I didn't feel any shift in her back muscles.

"You want to be a mother?" I wasn't trying to be combative, I really wanted to get to the bottom of her fixation on pregnancy.

"Yeah, I want a baby."

I thought of a small child having a tantrum to get a pretty doll. "Do you have sisters who have children?" I tried. I dialed my intention to loving, mothering energy flowing from my hands into her body as I worked.

"My younger sister already has two!" That felt like part of it —competition with the sister.

"And you feel like you're getting too old to have a baby?"

She didn't answer.

"How old are you?" I asked.

"Twenty-eight, three months ago."

I was startled again. That didn't seem old to me. It seemed young to be so frantic about it.

"What would you do if you really couldn't make a baby of your own?" I didn't sense that I should tell her I had been adopted.

She didn't say anything.

"Would you adopt a baby?"

"No. I want my *own* baby."

This told me that the issue wasn't motherhood. Somehow her ability to get pregnant was critical to her self-esteem. My guess was that it had to do with the politics in her family. Maybe her sister had given birth first, produced the first grandchildren, and she felt she had to compete for her parent's approval. Maybe the competition wasn't tacit. I asked about her parents and sister but she didn't want to talk about them.

So. Although I figured that her family's dynamics were at the core of her pregnancy issues, she didn't want to explore there. I knew enough about her will not to push it any further.

When my hand touched the curve of her lower back, I

suddenly got a clear vision of her with premature triplets, one with severe birth defects. I sensed she wouldn't want this. I understood this was like Scrooge's visit with the ghost of Christmas Future in Charles Dicken's *A Christmas Carol.* I was seeing the shadow of things that might come to pass if nothing changed.

Maybe she could physically get pregnant but was pinching the flow of energy so tightly she was subverting her own purpose. I massaged her legs in silence, letting the next move come to me. Her muscles were beginning to soften.

"I just got a vision of you as a mother." I said cautiously. "Maybe with more than one child."

She practically leaped up off the table in excitement. I had her turn over.

"I see you as a mother. What I feel in your body is not that you can't get pregnant but that you're trying so hard and your will is so fixed on getting pregnant that you've cut off the flow of energy. Becoming a mother is about a lot more than just getting pregnant. Pregnancy is just the first part of the huge process of parenthood. What about focusing on the baby you want to have. A healthy, beautiful baby, with you as its loving mother. You may even have more than one at a time, you have so many fertility hormones in your system. What do you think about twins?"

"I never thought about it."

"Well, it might help if you ease up a bit. You know the saying 'be careful what you wish for, you may get it'? You're focused only on pregnancy. But really, you want more than that."

"You're right."

"Hawaii is a very fertile place. I've had two babies here,

beautiful, healthy children at their timing, not mine. Children come when the time is right based on things we don't always know about. You have to trust."

She seemed so relieved. Her body was letting go on many levels. As I worked on her arms and face, she asked me about my children, about Hawaii. To finish, I gently stroked her hair.

"It'll be all right," I assured her. "Your body is young and healthy. Your husband loves you. Just let it come to you without force. Being a mother is wonderful. It's also a lot of work. And there's no going back once you've started. Focus on the person you want to parent for the rest of your life. If all you think about is getting out of the starting blocks, you won't be prepared for the rest of the race. Just let it flow."

She got up off the table saying, "Thank you so much! I feel so much better!" She looked over to her husband. "Honey, how was yours? Mine was great!"

I opened my arms and she grabbed me for a tight hug. "Remember, *Trust*," I said quietly into her ear. "It'll all work out." That felt true. I have not heard whether or not she eventually got pregnant and had babies. I trust that somehow Susan will find this book and contact me to let me know how it all turned out. I will let you know then, too.

EXERCISE 8: **Flexing Your Intuition**

You already are intuitive. But life in this busy, modern world tends to squeeze out your intuitive impulses and keep you locked in your rational mind. You have to invite back your intuition, welcome it when it shows up, and celebrate the riches it brings you.

1. Start keeping track of your intuitive insights. When you keep a dream journal, you invite in more dreams and your recall of them improves. In the same way, a separate "Intuition Journal" can invite in and reinforce your intuitive strength. Note serendipitous co-incidences like when you impulsively bring flowers to a friend for the first time and it turns out her dog died and you didn't even know the dog was sick. Or when you spontaneously take a different route to work and it turns out there was a traffic tie-up that you would have gotten stuck in had you gone your usual way. Note if you felt anything in your body such as lightness in your head, neck, or chest when you had the intuitive insight. Note any conditions that might have contributed to your intuitive openness such as whether you've had especially deep sleep the night before or good sex.

2. The point is not to quantify and chart out your experience, but to make connections and see how much intuition is always in play in your life. By appreciating and acknowledging your intuitive powers you will strengthen them.

3. Talk about your intuition with others. This will expand your range of experience and you are likely to hear some fascinating stories. Words like *spontaneous, impulsive, uncanny, insightful, perceptive, inspired, irrational-but-true, co-incidence, and serendipity* point to the intuitive.

4. Write down your predictions for yourself a month, a year, five and ten year into the future. If you have any predictions from the past, get them out and see how they have played out.

5.   Note the *"I knew it!"*'s in your life. Like when you know who's on the phone without seeing caller I.D. or you suddenly think of someone you haven't thought of in a while and then they call you. There are times when your mind guides you from experience, like when you know to bring a book to read when you pick up your son because soccer often finishes 20 minutes late. And there are instances when neither your mind nor experience could possibly know but your intuition guides you the right way.

The more you work with it, the stronger and surer you will be in your intuitive knowing.

CHAPTER 9

Coming into Alignment

*You draw from memory, from your understanding of life,
and others' understanding. All you've read and absorbed
falls like a jewel into your being.*

~ Martha Graham

People who find themselves on a healing quest often discover that the spiritual insights gained along the way
outweigh the pain and suffering. What they discover usually
puts the whole situation—and their lives—in a larger, more
beautiful context. As their perspective widens, they begin to
understand these "seemingly unknowable" or "sense-less"
events as part of a bigger picture.

The default blueprint for human development is to be born
a healthy baby with clean mental/emotional filters—no judgments, no positive or negative charge on the thoughts and
feelings, and all of the energy flowing unobstructed through
the body. A healthy baby breathes fully, and emotions don't get
"stuck." But that's just the prototype.

We all deviate in various ways, a little or a lot, from that blueprint. Those things that aren't "ideal" make us unique and give us our script in life. We choose our social, physical and environmental challenges—an alcoholic father, Down's syndrome, infertility, etc.—to learn certain lessons. One person gets "perfect" vision or "perfect pitch" but one leg is shorter than the other and is prone to skin problems. Another person experienced cancer as a kid and thereby developed the stamina and determination to climb mountains. Yet another lives with multiple sclerosis, which taught him the patience and compassion to rehabilitate wounded birds. The substance abuse counselors I know were once addicted themselves. No one gets *all* the "bad stuff" or *all* the "good stuff." It comes in a mixed package. Then with a healing intention and conscious work we can spin the gunk into gold.

When we were growing up, we didn't get all our needs met at every moment. Perhaps if we got all your needs met on time in just the right way, we would have no hang ups or insecurities, but we probably wouldn't be able to understand other people and their insecurities, either. We'd be isolated from the human experience. When our needs don't get met, we learn to deal with it; we learn to comfort ourselves; we learn how to respond to adversity; and we develop empathy for others who have suffered.

These next two stories illustrate the larger patterns of a person's life, how seemingly unrelated situations are really part of the healing journey. I tell them when I feel someone's predominant thought is: *It's not supposed to be this way.* Resistance to *what is* is the cornerstone of stress. See if you can use this story to recognize a situation in your life that you really don't like but that might be serving a bigger purpose for you.

The Young Widow

A woman in her early forties, let's call her Marion, came to me for a massage complaining of pain in her right shoulder. I remember being surprised that this woman's back was remarkably free of tension along her left side and in those back and shoulder areas where I usually find evidence of conflict in work or relationships. She didn't seem to be repressing her emotions, or have conflict about what she was *doing*. However, her right shoulder and upper traps felt gridlocked and nearly solid. I had never felt a tension pattern like that.

I kept working while probing gently for clues about how to work with this woman. I mentioned that I didn't feel the repressed sadness or the other things I usually feel in people's back. She told me that her husband had been killed in a helicopter crash two years before and she had then spent two years actively, consciously crying and letting go of her grief. She said she was pretty cried out.

I was getting a picture by then so I started pressing into the tightest spots on her right shoulder and asked, "So what's *this* about?" She told me that she had married late in her thirties, thrilled to be on the track of her dream family. "You know, I wanted the husband, the 2.2 children, the white picket fence and the dog." She said this facetiously but the bitterness in her voice and the feel of her muscles told me she meant it. "We had just started trying to get pregnant when he crashed."

"You feel angry and resentful," I confirmed.

"Oh, I know all about the grieving process. I'm writing a book about everything I've gone through. I know it will help other people deal with early and unexpected deaths. That's why my back is so clear. I've gone through every kind of therapy you can name: rebirthing, psychotherapy, massage and several others."

"Something's still got you though."

"Well I've gone through all the stages, disbelief, anger, sadness."

"So what is this?" I asked.

"I thought maybe it might be from the hotel mattress or the flight over." *Interesting*, I thought, *All that body-mind work and she went right back into the mind's explanation for her mysterious pain.*

I suspected I was probing into a blind spot so I wanted to be careful to speak in a way she could hear. "This tension is markedly on your right side. The right side is your thinking side, the mental side. If the issue was primarily emotional, it would probably show up on your left side. It's not the *feeling* that's unresolved or unexpressed, it's the *thought* about something." I paused to see if she would make the connection herself. Finally, I said, "Could it be the *thought* that this isn't the way it's supposed to be for you?"

"Yes!" she exploded, "I'm 41. He died when I was 39. That's too young to be a widow! We were just about to have a baby! I didn't even get a baby! I could've made it as a single mother."

"You signed up for the husband and the family and the white fence and right as you were about to close your hands on it, it got snatched from you. You've processed the emotions but you're stuck with the *thought* that this isn't the way it's supposed to be."

She calmed down as the truth of that settled in. "But I know he didn't intend to crash."

"He was the pilot?"

"Yeah, he'd been flying for twenty years."

"You can feel resentful of the situation you find yourself in without feeling resentful toward him, personally." I felt the clear spots in her back where most people have conflict-tension about their work. "Well, you don't have the kids and your perfect picture, at least not right now. But on some level you're very at peace."

"I know I'm supposed to be writing this book."

"Would you say that's your true calling?"

"I don't know, maybe the start of it. I have a lot to say to people about grief. I've been through so much."

I put my hand on her shoulder and felt that it had relaxed considerably. By this time I worked down her legs and I asked her to turn over. "And what about motherhood? There are lots of ways to be a mother."

"I've thought about adopting."

I felt that electric surge of recognition throughout my body (like goosebumps, but inside). I suddenly pictured a little boy, a brown boy with nappy blond hair who absolutely needed her love. I told her, "I just *got* the image of a little boy, about two years old, who's been through hell. He needs you." We both started crying with the energy of it. "Would you adopt a little black boy?"

"Absolutely." She gasped, "I see him too. Oh my God! I don't think my husband would have allowed it."

"I don't know what his name is or how you're going to find him, but he's waiting for you to come get him."

She sat bolt upright. I had the impression she would have rushed off the table to go find him that very instant. "I know where to go."

"To find your boy?!"

"Yeah, I have a pretty good idea."

"Do you know him already?"

"My boy." She wasn't really answering me but she said it with absolute peace and conviction.

We looked at each other, clearly struck by the intensity of the impression we both had. "That's *it*, isn't it? You are going to be that boy's mom." I said, smiling. "How's your shoulder?" I teared up then, I cried when I wrote it, and I still get goose bumps every time I reread this part of the story.

"It feels a lot better." She sounded surprised. She lay back down and we finished the massage.

As I was working on her forehead I said, "He's what this whole thing leads to."

"Yes, he is," she said, her gaze strong and purposeful.

After I'd finished and she was putting her bracelet back on, I said, "He's just the beginning." My heart felt very full.

She looked at me, as though for the first time. "Thank you," she said, and hugged me. Then her gaze got that purposeful look again, and I knew that little boy wouldn't have to wait much longer for his new mom to come love him.

The Woman with Stained Glass Eyes

Dana came to see me in her seventh month of pregnancy for her first-ever massage. She had the most striking eyes, multicolored and full of light—like stained glass windows. A demure young woman of mixed ancestry, she had just completed her first year working as a Hotel Assistant Manager and the hotel was treating her to a first-ever massage. I was surprised when she said she'd grown up on Molokai.

Molokai is a beautiful, quiet, sparsely populated island that is nothing if not relaxed and out-of-the way. Dana had the gentle unassuming manner I'd met before in Molokaians, but I knew that having lasted a year as a HAM, working long hours at the bottom of a heavy corporate ladder, belied an inner grit not associated with Molokai. When I put my hands on her shoulders, I felt as much tension as I often feel in shoulders that have just arrived from Manhattan.

I asked, "What's all this about? There's more than just pregnant-working-mom tension here."

"This is my first baby. My boyfriend's mom hates me. She calls me "the haole girl." *Ha'ole* literally means 'without breath' in Hawaiian. It is commonly used to mean white person or Caucasian, sometimes in a derogatory way.

"Haole?!" Dana 's glowing brown skin and almond shaped eyes didn't look very 'ha'ole' to me. "What's she?"

"She's Filipina. My father's German and Irish and my mother was Filpina, Hawaiian, Portugese, and Japanese."

"Wow, the complete mix. Your mother's not alive?" I asked.

"She died when I was two years old. Then I had a step-mother. She came from the mainland and forbade us to speak pidgin. We had to use proper English in the house, or else." (Not being allowed to speak pidgin on Molokai would be like a songbird being forbidden to sing in the forest.)

Remember the context here. I doubt she would have told me these things if we had just met and were standing together chatting socially. But she had literally taken off her outer trappings

REMIND ME NOT TO IMPULSE EAT

and I was pushing on the muscles that held her emotional memories. I was listening to her words and her muscles with complete focus, compassion, and a healing intention.

The layers of conflict I felt in her shoulders began to open apart. First there was the understandable worry about her first pregnancy. Next came the pain from her potential mother-in-law rejecting her for not being Filipina enough. Then there was pain from the step-mother rejecting so much that was a part of her. Underneath that was the pain of losing her mother so young—the core of the pain that kept replaying itself.

Her breathing was fast and shallow as she talked about these experiences that hurt her so profoundly. I coached her to breathe

193

deeply and allow herself to feel the emotions, the pain of rejection and abandonment, the loss of love. It took a few minutes for her to work into deep breaths but gradually she opened up. She started crying.

I sat her up, made sure the towel stayed wrapped around her and held her while she cried. We rocked a while in silence. When the wave of emotion had passed, she lay back down and we continued with the massage. After that kind of crying, you feel rung out, cleansed, like a husk has been removed.

As I finished the massage, she asked, "What was all that?"

"You want the psychology textbook version?"

"Sure," she said.

"You've been carrying the pain from repeated maternal rejection. The core wound is probably your mother's death. Even though you know she didn't deliberately abandon you, that's how it felt to you as a toddler. A little child would feel she wasn't worthy of a mom or she'd have stayed. On top of that your stepmother told you that everything about your mixed heritage is wrong, you're not white enough. Now your mother-in-law won't accept you because you're too white, not Filipina enough. That's a heavy load. But you can dump it. You've interpreted all that rejection to mean you are not worthy of love, that there's something wrong with you. You're beautiful, and capable, and loving, and strong—look at you! You can draw on the strength of several cultures and several gene pools. You can pick and choose the best from each, and it's all really you. As you step into motherhood, you have an opportunity to see how false the idea of unworthiness is. Do you think you have a boy or a girl?"

"A little girl."

"Well she's got a mixed background and you're going to love

her just the way she is, right? The way you deserve to be loved. You're already perfect to your baby, you know. She already loves you. That's unconditional love."

She smiled, sniffed back a tear, and nodded.

"When you feel tension in your shoulders, take a deep breath and check in to see if it's from the hotel crisis you just handled or from some feeling of unworthiness that's surfacing to be cleared. You *are* worthy. Just tune into that love that you feel and it'll blast away all that darkness. That's not your darkness. You are full of love. Love is right here in your belly coming to help you learn the lesson. In loving her, you will learn to extend that love to yourself.

"There's more sadness in there that's going to come up. You don't just melt twenty years of hurt in one massage. But now you see what's in there and how you can let it go, you're not stuck. Will you come get another massage sometime?"

Dana took my card saying she wanted to keep getting massages. To date I haven't worked on her again but I know she's had a beautiful baby and I know she's no longer completely trapped behind that wall of rejection. She's resilient and full of mettle. She knows that she can call me if she needs me. Sometimes that's enough.

If you have energetic blockage, pain or dysfunction, the first step is to acknowledge it. Sometimes the blockage simply dissipates once your conscious will recognizes it and allows energy to flow there. It can be that the energy from the attention of the conscious will is enough to initiate the energy moving through the area of blockage. In other words, the *intention* to recognize a problem is what starts the healing motion. Of course you prefer it when the pain goes away completely but it is just as much a victory if you thoroughly feel and accept your pain even if it doesn't all go away immediately. More energy is still flowing through that area than there was. The fact that some pain remains simply indicates that there is still further healing work to be done.

I have come to apply some of the things I was learning to my own body by taking more conscious care of it. I stopped eating red meat when I was thirteen, for example, which was tough in my carnivorous household. I experimented with my diet to find what worked best for my body and explored all sorts of medical and alternative remedies for my allergies and breathing problems. Over the years I've received lots of massage and peeled away my long-held emotional trauma layer by layer. I am getting physically and emotionally healthier even as I age because I'm also getting better at paying attention to my body's signals and responding with love. I still do not hear everything my body communicates. I have taken wrong turns that set me back, but I see it all as part of a healing journey. It's an evolutionary process. I continue to listen to see what my body will call for next.

Along the way, I've learned several of my body's specific signals that something is out of balance. For example, if I start to get a migraine headache, if my legs itch when I go into the ocean, or if my elimination decreases, I know I haven't been drinking enough water. If I re-hydrate myself, these symptoms go away. If I feel gas pains after eating, I know I ate too fast and gulped down air along with my food. I then use this as a guideline to pay attention to chewing and slow myself down while I eat. I can also tell my body needs vitamin C when my skin has a certain mushy feel to it; it feels like the cell membranes lack integrity. It doesn't take any kind of genius to learn these kinds of things about our own bodies. All we have to do is pay attention.

☯

When I loved myself enough I began to feel such relief.

~ Kim McMillen

There's a lot of talk these days about self-esteem and loving yourself. If we all genuinely loved ourselves at the very deepest level, we wouldn't criticize, complain or punish ourselves or others. We wouldn't be thinking the negative thoughts that become emotion and then physical disease. We would take the greatest care of ourselves and we would be kind and generous with others because our own deepest need is met and it feels good to act in loving ways. To love ourselves, we may simply need permission or to be shown what loving oneself looks like. Before I spend any more words about it, let's get to the heart of the matter.

You can easily diagnose if lack of self-love is an issue for you. Try this now: take a deep breath and say out loud (you can whisper) "I love myself." Keep deepening your breath and say it again, feeling internally as you say it. "I love myself." Do you smile and feel a flowing warmth in your body? Or does your breath catch and you feel uncomfortable? If you have trouble breathing deeply and saying with sincerity and conviction, "I love myself", you could probably use some self-lovin. Then again, couldn't we all?

The most effective way I know to convince yourself that you are worthy of love is to act loving toward yourself. Show yourself love. Treat yourself with the same kindness, understanding and generosity you would bestow on someone you were madly in love with.

I know wealthy parents who give their kids every conceivable toy and luxury but don't spend much time with their kids. The visible message is "You are worthy of all this *stuff*." The subtle message is, "You're not worthy of my time and attention." Which message do you think the body *gets* the most?

Bodies are literal, in-the-moment, animalistic. Your body wants physical, palpable demonstrations that you're lovable. It understands hugs and caresses and active nurturing as acts of love. It needs your time and attention. It wants you to listen to it and respond appropriately. And there's no better time than now to start practicing this.

EXERCISE 9: **Loving Your Body**

1. Take a deep breath. Take three more slow, full, deep breaths. That alone is a self-loving act.

2. Ask yourself: "Am I treating myself like someone I truly love?" Do I rest when I need to rest? Do I give myself enough water throughout the day and good food? Do I do self-destructive things like eat or shop to fill a nebulous void? What do I *really* want?" Give yourself the gift of true attention. If you answered "no" to some of those questions, the next question if "Why?" Be brutally honest with yourself and listen. Often, deep down, the answer is some version of: "I don't feel worthy" or "I want love." You can show your body love by giving it attention and good care and listening—whatever you didn't get up until now.

3.   Take yourself on occasional love-my-body dates. Take time out of your hectic schedule and put yourself first for one afternoon this week. Indulge your body. It doesn't have to be expensive. Get creative. Splurge on yourself with time or money in a way you usually don't. Allow yourself the luxury of a long hot bath—with yummy oil or bath salts. Epsom salt (magnesium sulfate) is fabulous for easing tension out of sore, tired muscles and you can get bath salts with feminine or masculine aromas. Get a massage or spend an hour stretching. Go on a long bike ride. Do something you don't usually do but know your body really needs. If you don't usually pleasure yourself (sexually), take time out to do that. Your body-mind will respond to the demonstration that you're worth the time and attention.

4.   Find a partner to support loving your body as a habit. For example, you can get massages at the same time or get them separately—but report back to each other. Start regularly walking or running or riding a bike with someone. Start going to a weekly yoga or tai chi class. The point is not necessarily to do your self-loving act with another person, but to have someone to support your showing love to yourself (and vice-versa.) It helps to have someone to brag to, share ideas with, and support you if you're flagging. This is a gift you can share.

5.   Of course the emphasis here is on the body but if you are being stingy with yourself in other areas that crimp your soul or reinforce a lack of self worth, show yourself love there, too. For me, this would mean putting aside time to make music. That desire is usually at the bottom of my to do list—but it's always on the list so I know it's important to me. Do a thorough inventory of ways you withhold nurturing from yourself and take steps to correct the pattern. This may sound easier said than done. If you wait until you feel worthy first, it may never happen. Act first, the intention and action will shift the feeling. You can start with small actions and build from there. You have permission. Just start.

If you don't feel particularly loving toward your body—fake it 'til you make it. Do loving things for your body anyway. Give it treats. Court your body as if it were a new lover. You will come to love it in the course of showing it love. As you learn to enlist your body as your truest life partner, you will wind up looking, feeling, and living better.

I once received an acupuncture treatment from a personally modest, financially independent man who had been practicing Chinese medicine for many years. When I asked him about his own health, presuming he had used his vast knowledge and resources to diagnose and "fix" his own troubles, he replied, "Oh, I have my little problems." I said, "But aren't you working to eliminate them?" "Well," he shrugged. "Let's say I've made peace with them." I was stunned. He certainly had the time and money to pursue any healing he wanted. This is what I felt held me back from being supremely healthy, not having the time and financial resources to seek *any* kind of healing help. He didn't want to do *everything possible*. He was not suffering over his suffering[18]. Rather than being eternally on a quest for more health, worrying about and making bigger problems out of his problems, he was quietly undergoing, and satisfied with the process. His example of loving acceptance of his own body and its little problems shines in my heart to this day. I think of my own "little problems" with more compassion as I remember his words and attitude of self-acceptance. I am always inspired when I see people, especially caregivers, taking good care of themselves. I love to meet healers who are in great health; they are walking the talk.

You cannot fix someone else's lack of self-love. You cannot love them so much it fills the place where their self-love belongs, but you can practice loving yourself and model that love for others to watch and emulate. This lesson was driven home to me in one moment several years ago. At my daughter's sixth birthday party, she wanted to cut and serve her own cake. She did a great job; she cut neat, even pieces, counted how many guests she had, and divided the cake accordingly. After she had served the last piece, she looked down at the empty platter

---

18   From its origin, *to suffer* simply means "to *undergo*".

and realized she hadn't allotted any for herself. She looked up at me with a quiver in her lower lip and said "Mom! There isn't any left for me!"

Understanding hit me like a bolt of lightening to the forehead. At that moment, I realized that I had not taught my daughter to count herself among those she gave of herself to, to save some of her resources for herself. I had modeled NOT counting myself in. I ran myself to exhaustion taking care of everyone else but myself—just as my (social worker) mother had done and her (nurse) mother before her. Seeing my daughter do the same thing made it clear that the pattern had to stop—immediately, and with me. I had *told* her to take care of herself, but without taking care of myself and showing her how, telling her obviously meant nothing. I could teach her best by example. Since that time, I do my best to rest when I'm tired; to give to myself as well as to others; and to count myself in when divvying out life's cake. I still have a ways to go at this but I'm getting better at it. Like everything I'm talking about here, it takes practice.

If we judge our bodies as inappropriate or gross we stem the flow of love and acceptance that results in healing. Advertisers tell us our body's odors are offensive and we must deodorize them. The media tell us that we are not beautiful with small breasts or an asymmetrical nose or a bald head, and we pay millions of dollars for cosmetic surgery to "fix" what is not broken. The more we buy into the external message that our bodies are not right just as they are, the more we lose access to the internal information that will help us be the healthiest we can be. We can reverse the momentum of defensive tension with self-love, gentleness, compassion, and patience.

When I feel a heavy dose of self-judgement in a person's body I often tell my version of Aesop's fable, The Wind and the Sun, to illustrate how gentleness can be more effective than force.

The Wind and the Sun

One day the Wind looked down and noticed a magnificently clad man riding a beautiful white stallion. The rider sat tall and straight in his gold-trimmed saddle and wore a richly embroidered scarlet cloak. The Wind called to the Sun, "Look at that! Such pride. I bet you I can part him from his fancy cloak." The Sun said, "You? With your blustering? I can do it before you. We'll both try, in our own way. You can even go first."

The Wind began to blow, harder and harder. But the rider fastened the clasps on his cloak and rode on. The Wind became angry and blew up a gale. The rider clutched the cloak even more tightly around himself and spurred his horse away from the Wind. As the Wind swelled to blow the rider off his horse, the Sun intervened saying, "That's enough. Now it's my turn." The Wind backed off with a smirk, confident that the rider wouldn't give up his cloak to the Sun, either.

The Sun shone gently down. The rider straightened from his battle against the wind and relaxed his grip on his cloak. As the Sun continued to shine, the rider grew warm and unfastened his cloak. The Sun gradually and patiently increased the heat until the man grew so warm he took off the cloak and put it away in his pack. The Sun won his bet with the Wind, demonstrating that gentleness and patience can penetrate where no amount of force can.

The following story is an illustration of that realization coming home to a man who was denying himself what he needed to be joyful.

Poet at the Foot of Kings

One Saturday, a close friend called saying her friend Gupta was in town briefly, en route to a job in the Far East. He was married with two kids and was under a lot of stress from his heavy-duty job as a governmental diplomat. He needed a massage, and she hoped I could do it. My friend agreed to watch my young kids while I worked on Gupta, and they came right over.

As I started the massage, the first strong intuitive impression I got was at the back of his heart. I pictured a man in a long white robe and white turban. I intuitively checked in to see if I was to say something. I got no impulse to keep quiet so I simply described the person I saw "in his heart."

He said, "That's how my father always dressed."

I asked him how he felt about his father, and nothing particularly negative (anger, fear, repressed emotion, etc.) came up. He said he had been close to his father and that he had passed on. What I felt may have simply been the love he has for his father that keeps him alive in his heart. I felt no need to pursue it further.

While I worked, I asked questions about the nature of the stress in his life. I felt various tense spots, but I did not get a sense of the main dynamic. When I had massaged a while more and sensed he was feeling comfortable, I returned to the areas just below his shoulder blades. I found tight knots there that felt charged with emotional energy.

As I pressed on the energetic knots, I said, "You feel that tension?"

"Yeah," he grunted.

"Can you breathe into it?" I asked. He did. "Does it feel any different when you do?" He nodded as the energy continued moving.

This spot is where I often find conflict between a person's various roles—son, brother, husband, dad, employee, student, boss, etc.—and his soul's purpose, what he's really here on earth to do and be. It's all that stuff one is *supposed* to do, *supposed* to be. A classic example of a perceived conflict between higher purpose and role in daily life would be the artist who waits tables for a living and does not make his artwork.

"Gupta," I asked suddenly, "What are you *really*?" I was surprised by my own question. I was impressed by Gupta's career and would not have imagined he was not fulfilled by it. He was living a life I had imagined for myself.

The question seemed to catch him off guard as well. The words, "I'm really a poet!" tumbled out with a startled sob.

"You know," he continued after a pause, "Poets used to be honored. They sat at the foot of kings and helped them rule with wisdom, from the heart."

"Do you write poetry?"

"I haven't written a poem in fifteen years."

"Why not?!" I asked, feeling energy flowing through the areas under my hands.

"Oh, I don't know. What's the point? When do I have the time? First there was my career and now my family. I spend most of my time working and traveling between assignments. Then when I'm home, I just want to be with my children. I just don't have the time."

We talked about poetry and discussed our favorite poets. He said he enjoyed his job, but it didn't feed his soul. I asked whether being recognized as a poet was an important part of his desire. He said that he preferred to write for himself and maybe a few others who *got* his poetry, but that he didn't necessarily want to publish. He said his poems weren't very mainstream.

"Recognition is the tricky part. If you just need to write poetry, that's easy!" I said. I could feel he did not agree with this. "When you're traveling between assignments—on the planes, in airports—what do you do?" I asked.

"I do work. Sometimes I read."

"But *there's* your time to write poetry, at least to start. How long is your flight tomorrow?"

"Nine hours," he said.

"Nine largely uninterrupted hours! You can write a decent poem or two in that time, surely. I know it's hard to turn on creative juices within a tight schedule, but it gets easier with practice. Can you at least start?"

"It's just not that simple."

"Why not? You just told me you are a poet. Poets write poetry. Make it a higher priority and you will find the time. Give yourself permission. Give yourself permission to write lousy poetry to start. You're in training again, after all. And you have nine glorious poetry-writing hours tomorrow." We continued talking about ways he could make more time for poetry writing.

The point was, he had gone in and visited a deeply-held frustration and breathed some energy into it. I did not tell him he was silly or that he should suppress it. I simply mirrored what he had said himself—"I'm a poet." That would not have happened if I had not found his spot, pushed on it and said, "What's this!?" I would not have just met him and found out, within fifteen min-utes, that his deepest unfulfilled longing was to write poetry. We have social defenses to prevent that sort of thing, after all. The act of taking off his clothes and lying down, bare and vulnerable, to offer up his tension set the stage for something unusual to happen. And in that vulnerable state, meeting a non-judgmental and loving witness with intuitive access to information about what was troubling him opened the way for healing. And Gupta loved himself enough to follow through.

In the following months, Gupta sent me several poems. They're actually quite good. Of course he's a poet! He has since written articles that have been published in national newspapers and is considering publishing a small anthology of his poems. I am honored to receive these poems and to have been present at the re-ignition point for his poetic creativity.

The Power of a Deadly Thought

Another time, I got a call from a friend saying her sister was coming to Maui for a visit. I had met the sister, Rebecca, once before. She was a corporate lawyer in her late 40s and the mother of a 3-year-old. She had been diagnosed with a malignant and aggressive tumor in the frontal lobe of her brain, right at the third eye, and had been given six weeks to live.

If I had received the phone call even two weeks earlier, I would have wondered what I could possibly do that would make any difference. I thought that cancer was a serious disease that took time to manifest and would take some time to heal—certainly longer than a fast-growing tumor would allow. But I had just read *Conversations with God; Book 1,* by Donald Neale Walsch[19] and I had a new understanding of how instantaneous healing is possible.

I was accustomed to seeing time as an expanded spiral (like a coil seen from the side, in two dimensions) and if events happen along that spiral, there isn't room for so much to happen in an instant. This is akin to looking at a puzzle from an angle where you can't see the solution. But if I looked down that spiral from the top—in effect rotating the puzzle to see two dimensions, but knowing there's a third dimension, depth —I could see that any point on what now appeared as a two-dimensional circle will belong to any number of cycles in three dimensions. I may not be physically able to see what goes on in the additional dimensions, but that does not mean that nothing is going on. So in the case of healing over time, I may not *see* the fourth (temporal) dimension, but I understand that there can be a lot going on at other levels that I can not sense directly.

I believed that if I could shift her belief as well, she could heal spontaneously. I knew enough of Rebecca's analytical, tough-willed nature to know I couldn't pussyfoot around with her. This was serious, and she had to *get* it, fast.

Once she was prone on the table, breathing, and I had checked in with my hands, I asked her, "Do you want to die?"

She was silent for a moment then launched into a saga of an unfulfilled and frustrated life. The father of her daughter (she was not married) was a problem. The house they were

---

19   Walsch, Donald Neale. *Conversations with God, Book I,* (Putnam, 1996)

remodeling was a problem. Her job, finances, and childhood wounds were problems. I agreed she had a lot on her plate, but none of her problems seemed insurmountable or life-threatening to me. While my hands worked, I pointed out that otherwise she was a healthy, intelligent, fortunate woman with a beautiful daughter, a supportive extended family, and good prospects. There was nothing I could see that warranted the decision to check out of her life.

I asked, "What about Sarah? (her daughter) Didn't you make a contract to be her mother? Was the contract to last for three years, then she would grow up with the pain of a mother who died when she was three?" I paused. "Is Roy (the girl's father) the man you want to be her most important influence growing up? He would be, if you died now."

I knew these questions would hit deep. The way I perceived it, this powerful woman had willed an end to her troubles without fully weighing the ramifications of her choice. She had made an emotional decision without her usual analyses. She was silent while she thought about this.

I told her about my realization about the nature of time from *Conversations with God*. I told her, "I believe in the possibility of healing your brain tumor, now, in this instant. I offer you that opportunity. But you have to want to live. You have to decide that your love for your own life and your love for Sarah is greater than the frustration and anger and sadness you feel about all the other things you mentioned." There was the rub—love for her own life, her own self.

I felt strong energy in the room and flowing through both of us. Rebecca was crying. I kept kneading the tense spots. By the time she turned over and I had worked up to her head, the energy there was not hard or concentrated. I felt energetic disturbance around her third eye but it felt penetrable, not like the knot of a tumor.

I asked her again, "Do you want to live?"

She said, "Yes, I think so. I'm scared."

"Scared to see all this for what it is, your own creation? Your life as the sum of all your choices?"

"Yes."

"Think of Sarah and how much you love her. Picture her face as she swung high into the air, the first time she could pump herself on a swing. Think of her losing her first tooth, then dressed for her first prom. Do you want to be there to see those things?" She nodded. "Do you choose to be Sarah's mother through her life?"

"Yes," she said.

"Can you extend the love you feel for Sarah to yourself? Do you choose to live your life, now?"

Sounding stronger, she said, "Yes."

"This tumor can dissolve in an instant. It manifested quickly, by your thought and will. It can dissolve that same way, now, immediately. With the help of God and the Universe. Now." I got the urge and clapped my hands together dramatically.

Well, I didn't feel the earth shake or see the walls fly apart from a bolt of lightning. We finished the massage and Rebecca got up and went on her way. I wasn't sure how much of it "took," but it certainly *felt* powerful.

She came back for a massage a few days later. This time I felt more energy moving through her. I repeated some of the things I had said the first time, but mainly she led the conversation. She seemed more confident, poised, and open than the previous time. It didn't feel like I was working on a woman who was going to die.

A few weeks later Rebecca called me from the mainland. She told me that after Maui, she had also gone to see a healer she had heard about in Sedona, Arizona. She had just seen the results of the latest CAT scan. There was no trace of a tumor. Having no other explanation, the doctors decided they must have been mistaken in their original diagnosis.

Now, I do not feel I healed her. I feel I helped catalyze the flow of energy for her use. It is as if I pulled out the necessary few sticks to unleash the logjam. My hands helped me find the sticks, and my intuition told me when and how to yank them. She then took her healing into her own hands because she had connected into the love in her life—for her daughter, her family, and finally, herself.

When you love yourself completely, you see your flaws and insecurities and blemishes and sins, and you love yourself anyway. You dig through the layers of guilt and shame and come to see that you are not uglier or less loveable than anyone else. As you allow in that deep love for your self, you find it easier to love those around you. You are loveable and so is your neighbor. They have flaws; you have flaws. They have strengths and talents; so do you. You recognize yourself and everyone you meet as a master in the making. As love of self inspires them you will make healthier choices in all aspects of your life—how you breathe, exercise, speak; how you spend your time and whom you spend it with. This is the golden nugget you get when you come to terms with and release the issues in your tissues.

CHAPTER 10

Healing Is a Practice Sport

Once we recognize what we are feeling, once we recognize we can feel deeply, love deeply, can feel joy, then we will demand that all parts of our lives produce that kind of feeling.

~ Audre Lourde

The primary goal of my work is to teach my clients to tune into their own bodies and recognize what they find there. It's easier to have someone guide you through the process as you are learning it, but eventually you want to understand your body's language on your own, without relying on an interpreter. You, Dear Reader, can learn your body's language on your own without my ever touching you. You can do this by setting the stage for a healing session where you are both healer and client. You can use it for a specific physical or emotional issue or simply when you feel out of balance and you're not sure exactly why. Add anything you want, but don't omit anything until you've tried it all at least once. Of course, you should work within the parameters of what you are physically capable and medically (and intuitively) advised to do.

The following is my method to tune in and listen to my body. I do this when I recognize I need healing. I enjoy receiving and learning from all kinds of healers, but this works when there's no one handy to work at the level I feel I need help. Plus, it's convenient, free, and empowering.

EXERCISE 10: **The Do-It-Yourself Healing Session**

STEP 1—**Make the time.** The first and probably most important step is to set aside specific time for healing and paying attention to your body. This declares and demonstrates your intention to heal. Make a formal appointment with yourself that you can look forward to. Write it down on your calendar.

STEP 2—**Clear the deck.** Turn off the phone and make yourself unavailable to any outside demands. It's ideal to be home alone or in a special quiet, natural place if you can, but simply quiet behind a closed (locked) door works too. Uninterrupted privacy is critical for being able to let down your internal defenses. You may have to make a deal with people you live with to achieve privacy at your house. Going to a friend's house can be another option.

STEP 3—**Prepare the space.** You can put on soft music, light candles or incense and do anything else that sets a mood of relaxation and peace for you. Candles are especially appropriate as they emit a *yin* light and give a lovely definition to the receptive mood you want to create.

Shower or bathe; put on loose, comfortable clothes (or leave them off); and generally prepare yourself the way you would for a massage. Move any furniture aside to create an area where you can move around freely. You can spread a mat, towels or blankets on a hard floor or a sheet on carpet. Bring in any pillows or gadgets you might need. Make sure you start to prepare yourself as you do all this by softening your mood and slowing down. Breathe fully. Leave the busy-ness behind. (If this sounds like you're preparing to make love, you're not too far off. In this case though, you are both lover and loved, and it's not about sex.)

STEP 4—**Tune in.** Sit or lie comfortably on the floor. Use pillows to support yourself so you can relax completely. Close your eyes and breathe deeply. Feel your body from the inside. Notice where the breath goes and where it doesn't go. Scan your entire body with your attention. Take plenty of time. I usually start from my toes and work upward, but head to toe works just as well. As you scan your body, explore what you find. Move around gently. Flex your toes, tighten and release, shake or stretch any part that feels stiff. If you feel tension anywhere, breathe into that area and do what it asks you to do to help it loosen. Stay focused on what you feel from inside. At the jaw, for example, open your mouth wide and move it from side to side. Stick out your tongue—hard. Go to the extreme of your movement. Scrunch up your lips. Play around. This should take time: twenty minutes to half an hour (ten minutes at the *least*). If you rush through it the first time, resolve to do it more slowly the next time or go back and do it again.

STEP 5—**Work with yourself.** At this point, you are probably aware of areas of tension that didn't simply shake out with a gentle movement. While focusing on any area that calls to you, gently roll around, twist, stretch, reach— whatever your body urges you to do to bring itself back into balance and alignment. I like to raise one knee and fold it over my other leg to twist my spine. Often a vertebra or two will adjust into place with a small "click". It is critical to continue to pay attention, breathe and move slowly so you don't hurt yourself.

Don't be shy. This is your body and your opportunity to get better acquainted with it in this way. Massage areas that are sore. Do whatever you need to help your body feel better. Getting up is fine as long as you stay focused on this process. Use props. I have a home-made metal **S** with wooden knobs on the ends as well as that store-bought, cane-like gadget[20] to help me put pressure into hard-to-reach spots in my back. You could also use an umbrella handle or a walking cane. You can lean into a doorjamb to work out the tension along your spine. It's amazing what you can find around the house to help. Be creative. In order to use any tool or gadget most effectively and avoid hurting yourself, make your body receptive by relaxing and focusing on what you are doing.

Let's say you find a tight spot in the middle of your back and your neck is stiff. For a tight spot in the middle of your back, you can lie or roll on a tennis ball; or use a marble,

---

20   For more information about the one I use, visit www.theracane.com

golf ball, or smooth stone (perhaps surrounded by pillows to cushion the lump) to put pressure on a sore spot behind the shoulders. To work on your neck, lie flat on your back (on a soft surface, with a cushion under your knees) so your neck doesn't have to do the work of supporting a heavy head while you're asking it to relax. Use your left hand to work on the right side of your neck and then your right hand to work on the left side of your neck. Breathe deeply and feel your way through the tension as you go. For any other areas that are hard to reach or need support, listen internally and experiment until you figure out a way to get the twist or pressure or stretch your body seems to want.

Do what your body tells you to do for it, even if it doesn't make logical sense. If you get the urge to sing or cry or yell, do it. There is no right or wrong in this. Just don't shut yourself down, don't censor yourself. If you find yourself remembering someone or some situation you haven't thought about in a long time, invite the memories, run the film. Stay with those thoughts and images to see what new insights you can gain about them. When you are in this tuned-in, self-aware state, whatever you do for yourself will be appropriate. When you get to the end of one issue or sequence, ask out loud or to yourself, "Is there anything else I need to explore at this time?" Keep going until you feel completely played out.

STEP 6—**Close.** If you've stayed tuned-in, there will come a point when you feel finished. The symphony has de-crescendoed, returned to tonic and the music stops.

At this point, breathe deeply and allow yourself to feel grateful and whole. You can bow, or say "amen", or do something that signifies grateful closure to you. Move slowly. Drink some water. Blow out any candles you've lit and follow any urges you have to write or draw or do something nurturing for yourself.

I remember finishing a session like this and feeling a strong urge to call an old friend I hadn't spoken with in some time. It turned out she was upset with me about something I didn't even realize I had done, and I was in such a soft, receptive mood, I could hear her complaint without becoming defensive. We were both happy to resolve the issue and get on with our friendship.

STEP 7—**Ongoing exercises.** There are many things you can do to cultivate the kind of awareness I've been talking about. When you find yourself waiting, breathe. In the doctor's waiting room, in traffic, in a meeting, in the airport—anytime your mind would wander or start spinning, bring your attention inward and use that time to practice tuning in to your body's communication and relax.

The next time you're in a loose crowd of people—at a mall, at a concert, at a conference, on campus—watch other people. (I recommend doing this around people you don't know so that it's easier to remain emotionally neutral and without judgment.) Notice their posture, their stride (or gait or shuffle) and their expression. Notice how that man's jaw juts forward and his shoulders hang back. Notice how hard that woman has to work just to carry herself forward with that much weight on her bones; watch how she favors her left leg. Observe all the ways a person's body seems to be communicating something. Practice reading body language without judgment. Imagine what it feels like to walk around in that man's glorious strong physique, and in that body that is shriveled and spent. Look closely and see if you get an impression of why those shoulders might be hunched forward or why that walk is so tight and clipped. Bodies transmit signals that communicate how they are interacting with the world. One body will demonstrate that, "I'm constantly ready to ward off attack"; another will give the impression, "I'm carrying the burdens of the world." This is the kind of listening I'm talking about—in this exercise, you're just listening to a body other than your own.

Use all of your senses to pay attention to physical signals—*without judgment*. When you shake someone's hand, pay attention to what signals you receive. Is the hand warm? Dry? Is the embrace crushing? Brief? Is the other person paying attention to your hand? Observe these things without *thinking* what this information means for *you*. Don't take it personally. What does the way someone smells tell you about his diet? Grooming? Anxiety level? Stay emotionally neutral. If you think "stinky", that's a judgment and you start off on a tangent about what *you* think about stinky people. Just notice and remain neutral. Listen to people's voices. You can hear if the energy flows strongly through their throat, if there's nasal tension or if they like speaking.

By now, you've gotten the idea that I'm talking about neutral observation, in real time. Here and now. Not comparing what you observe to anything in your past or your emotional memory bank. No judgements such as, "He could stand to lose a hundred pounds" or "She looks so uptight." Quietly observing is right-brain territory, and it is a lovely counterbalance to all the judging and worrying you do. Try these exercises and then invent your own. At first it might be easier to observe other people without judgment than to observe yourself without judgment. You can then shift your skill and ease with this kind of observation to your own body. Do those tense shoulders remind you of yours? Imagine what would happen if that man took a deep breath and allowed his shoulders to relax and drop. What would happen if you did that? You can learn a lot by observing other people, and then apply the insight gained to your own body.

Additional ideas:

Check inside throughout your day. Get into the habit of checking in with your body when you've been concentrating on a task for any length of time. Is your face pinched into a grimace as you concentrate? Is your stomach knotted? Your jaw clenched? *Are you breathing?* If you're late for an appointment and driving fast, are your thighs tight and your head thrust forward like a racehorse fleeing the crop? These are things you do unconsciously that steal energy from your smooth functioning and leave you tense and tired. When you notice those tightly held areas where energy and breath isn't flowing, breathe deeply and allow your breath to reenergize them. You'll feel much better.

Observe yourself. Look at photos of yourself or—better yet—a video tape of yourself in movement, walking, running, and interacting with others. Observe yourself non-judgmentally, the way I described doing with other people. Is that the way you normally stand or sit or walk? What does your posture say about how you were feeling? How are you holding your shoulders, neck and hips? For example, I once noticed in photos of myself holding infants that my shoulder holding the baby was tightened nearly up to my ear. The next time I held an infant I paid attention to my shoulders and released the tension I didn't need simply to support the baby. The baby was more comfortable and so was I.

Watch how you eat. Do you take time to feed yourself nourishing food? Do you take the time to really taste it and chew it well? If you experience any digestive distress, notice if you gulp your food, swallowing down air as you eat. As a child you may have been told to chew a certain number of times before swallowing. The point is not to compulsively count as you eat but to get into the habit of chewing your food thoroughly. Digestion starts when you mix the food with the enzymes in your saliva as you chew. How you feel as you eat affects digestion as well.

Treat yourself well. Start looking for simple, nourishing ways to relax and do nice things for yourself. When you come home from work (or any time you feel tired and tense) instead of reaching for alcohol or the TV, warm up wet towels and put them on your face and neck or feet and hands.

THE GOOD NEWS FOR YOU IS THAT YOU'RE FIT AS A FIDDLE.
THE BAD NEWS FOR US IS THAT WE HAVE NO IDEA HOW
YOU DID IT.

To do this you can wet a hand towel (or clean, absorbent dish towel), squeeze out the excess water, and heat it in a microwave oven. You can also heat water on the stove, then dip the towel(s) in the hot water and wring out the excess. You want the water hot enough to make the towels steamy but not hot enough to burn you. It's amazing how quick this is to do after you have done it once—and it works wonders to relieve stress and bring you back to your center after a hard day's work. When I do this, I reheat the towels and reapply them two or three times. Sometimes I put a drop or two of lavender essential oil on the wet towel. Sometimes I go all out and give myself a full facial with a clay mask since the steam from the towels has already opened my pores and I'm already in self-treat mode. There are dozens of simple ways to treat yourself once you start thinking in these terms.

Once you have interrupted the after-work TV or drinking habit, it's easier to hear your body telling you to go for a walk, ride your bike, or somehow get some exercise. Your body will help you get what you need for greater balance if you give it the chance. The hardest part is overcoming inertia to get started.

A hot bath is also great for relieving stress and tension. In our culture men don't generally take baths, but they do not need to miss out on such a great relaxing opportunity. You can use yummy-smelling bath salts and oils to make your bath more delightful. For starters, simply squirting liquid dish soap into the running water makes an instant bubble bath. Try it!

Dance. Most of us don't do it enough. It works wonders to loosen up the hips and release the pent-up energy that coagulates in our butts from sitting too much. Dancing is part of our heritage as humans. You may not consider yourself good at it, but I bet you enjoy yourself if the conditions are right. All you need is space to move and *your* music.

I don't go out dancing as much as I used to, but that doesn't stop me from dancing. I clear the middle of the living room, play music that gets me moving, and go for it. Sometimes my kids join me. I prefer to do it when I have the house to myself and I can turn the music up and let myself go wild. I tune in to the way my body needs to move and get a good sweat going. I always feel better afterward. I can't recommend it enough.

There is no end to the ways you can be kind to yourself if you give yourself permission. If you tend to be stingy with yourself, denying yourself relaxation and pleasure because subconsciously you don't feel you deserve kind treatment —shift that thought. You are loveable. You are worthy. Love yourself. Practice being kind to yourself. If you were told (or shown) that taking care of yourself in kind and loving ways is weak or sinful, change that thought. Reversing the behavior fills the void left by the lack of loving attention and resets the ability to receive. If you treat yourself *as if* you felt worthy, you will begin to transform your (erroneous) perception of unworthiness to one of self-love and acceptance. As you take better care of yourself you become better able to take care of others as well.

There are many things you can do to give yourself a tune-up. Rest tops the list; laughing is key and helps you relax, so does exercise. Getting a massage can serve as a tune-up—helping you to breathe better, to release accumulated tension, and to identify the parts of your body that have experienced unusual wear and tear and need additional care —much as going to the dentist helps you do that with your teeth. Yoga, tai chi, and regular meditation are all practices that can teach you to recognize tension, and help alleviate it when you do find it. Where else in our culture do we get this kind of training? We usually don't learn anything like this in school. Nor did most of our parents show us how to take this kind of care of our bodies.

If I were to design a general minimum health maintenance guide it would say:

- Breath deeply to fill the entire lungs. **When in doubt, stick your belly out** to restart the natural breathing mechanism.

- Retrain yourself to breathe into tension rather than clenching into it.

- Drink plenty of water. The standard recommendation used to be eight 8oz. glasses of water per day. I would add two glasses for each alcoholic drink, plus extra glasses for prescription medication or vitamins, air travel, exercise, and anything else that dehydrates the body.

- Get a massage once a week. Twice per month is OK. Once a month is the minimum to lower your overall tension level. Pay attention internally and breathe while on the table.

- Do Yoga, Tai Chi, Chi Kung or some practice that helps you slow down, turn inward, pay attention to your body, and move breath/energy.

- Get regular, aerobic exercise.

- Eat clean, fresh, unprocessed foods.

- Investigate the emotional components of the stress and tension in your life.

- Look for ways to welcome your intuition into your life.

- Work on forgiving anyone or any situation that causes you pain. Take action to correct mistakes you've made with people. Forgive yourself for anything you still feel bad about.

- Treat yourself as if you are your own true beloved. The more you do this, the more you will treat others with this love as well.

Self-loving acts can be an easy, relatively inexpensive, and welcome part of your daily life. The challenge is simply to do them. Put away your inhibitions and ignore that voice that says, "But *I* don't do that . . ." or "But I don't have the time . . ." You'll never 'find' the time as if it's sitting on a shelf somewhere, just *do* something nurturing for yourself. Start. Begin. Call for a massage appointment or go through the tuning inward sequence I just outlined. If you have read this far, you are probably ready to act on it.

Pavlov Was Right

I had a regular massage client who was using massage to help him overcome drug addiction. After the first few sessions, he began to request the same music every time to accompany his massage. It was a cassette that I had made with two Windham Hill sampler albums, 1992 on one side and 1996 on the other. It became such a part of our routine that over the next two years I automatically put on the tape every time he came.

When the time came for him to leave the island, he came for a farewell massage. I gave him the tape with my blessings.

A few months later he called me from Texas to say that when he felt like he needed a massage, he would turn the lights low, lie down and listen to the tape I gave him. He would breathe deeply and relax his muscles to the music he had heard so often, like the dogs Ivan Pavlov trained to associate eating time with the sound of a bell. He told me that afterwards he felt about 80 percent as refreshed as if he'd actually come to see me for a massage. Of course the touch and the personal interaction was missing, but he had learned to take time out for relaxation, breathe deeply, and then listen to his body and release the tension he felt there. He had learned the tools and was taking the time to fix it himself!

Jilted Bill

Among the many people I've worked on over the years, Bill stands out in my mind as particularly healthy and balanced. He was 45, fit, said he ran his own successful telecommunications company, and had two great kids and a loving relationship with his wife. He swam, played soccer, did yoga, drank plenty of water and ate cleanly. He got a massage regularly and didn't have muscular knots, aches, or pains. He seemed to have everything in balance: family life, inner life, work, play, and health. I can't think of any (adult) body I've ever massaged that seemed as in-balance.

Many people tell me 'everything's fine' and then I put my hands on their body and feel a different story. In his case though, his relaxed, healthy muscles, bore out everything he said. From a massage point of view, his body didn't *need* much. Getting a massage on vacation was just part of his program to keep things in balance.

Though the area wasn't what I call screaming, I did keep coming back to the area in his back behind his heart. I held my hand over that area and a *knowing* feeling came to me: he was jilted as a teenager, and it hurt him tremendously, still.

Now I admit this wouldn't normally be a huge psychic leap. I could probably root around and find some heartache during most everyone's adolescence. But in his case, it felt like he had cleared himself of most of the emotional trauma that people commonly carry as energetic knots in their muscles—except this one. This knot may have been one of the last ones on the rope, so to speak. And I wouldn't have felt the issue so clearly if it wasn't surfacing for some attention. I asked him if he wanted to explore any issues I might find. He did.

I said, "I feel something here, in the back of your heart. You were a teenager. She jilted you." I felt rather than saw a rueful smile and knew I had hit the mark.

He picked his head up from the face cradle and said, "That was a long time ago."

"But it's still here ," I pressed.

"That was a long time ago," he insisted.

I said, "But we're both feeling it now, in your back." He smiled again. "What was her name?"

"Peggy." He paused. "Jeez, that was a long time ago."

"And the hurt?" I felt around for a response. I clearly got the impulse to pursue it. "Could you have a dream tonight, in which you rewrite the ending? Make it come out so it doesn't hurt so much? Not that you walk off hand in hand into the sunset. That didn't happen. But have a talk with that heartsore guy you were back then. Tell him he's not unworthy and let him know he will love again. And then give it a more satisfying ending somehow, for both of you. You're clearly better off now."

He nodded and I continued on with the massage.

I don't know whether Bill acted on that suggestion. That old wound certainly hadn't prevented him from building a wonderful life. But it did present itself to be cleared. I tell that story to people to make the point that even otherwise balanced, fulfilled people have old wounds and multiple layers of long-held pain. As long as we're alive, we have issues to work on. With practice and attention though, it gets much easier.

☯

In Conclusion

As I close a healing session, I am usually seated by my client's head. I take a few deep breaths and ask my client to do the same if she is not already doing so. I close my eyes as I stroke her hair and forehead and say a little prayer of thanks for the opportunity to work on her and myself. I might call for balance or bring in a little extra light energy. (I think in terms of God's blessing and God's love if I know those are her terms). What this all boils down to is reconnecting with Spirit and the God-like part of ourselves. The closing is the acknowledgement and thanks for whatever divine help has come forth, the *amen* or "so be it" at the end of a prayer.

Throughout this book I have been talking about reconnecting the wholeness you were born to—in mind, body, emotion, and spirit—enlarging the feeling of love to encompass your own body the way a loving mother cares for her newborn. This means listening to your body and treating it with love. As you practice loving yourself, you will reestablish a balance between the needs of the mind, the emotions, the body, and the spirit. My hope is that as you reconnect with your own body in a loving way, you will begin to see that taking care of yourself and each other and our earth are all extensions of the same process.

Even if you are aware of non-physical origins of your physical problems, you may need another person to offer a different perspective and help release the stuck energy. John Donne was right, "No man is an island." We are all here to learn from each other and help each other. Nothing replaces the value of human touch or the magic between a healer and a receptive body.

If you take nothing else away from this book, take the idea that you have to address the emotional aspects of your illness to heal it completely. I'd like you to remember that you will be more effective if you breathe into tension than if you clench into it. I would also like you to pay attention to your body and drink plenty of water. Get a massage and pay attention to your breath during it—even if the therapist doesn't specifically tell you to. Slow down. Listen to your body. Use the ideas in this book. Read other books. If you don't find the answer you need from one source, keep looking until you do find your answer. Try the exercises from the *On Your Own* section. And breathe, breathe, breathe. **When in doubt, stick your belly out!**

I wish you joy and courage on your healing journey.

To know even one life has breathed easier because you have lived. This is to have succeeded.

~ Ralph Waldo Emerson

If you are finished with this book, please pass it to a friend. It does not help anyone sitting on a shelf.

Recommended Resources

The following list includes titles of the books I refer to most often in my work with other people and with myself. Each book contains healing insights, tools, or medicine to help you in your quest for greater well-being. And like other remedies, they help most when you get the right one for you at the right time.

The list is meant to give you a nudge, if you need one, not be a definitive guide. I offer title, author, publication date of the copy I have, and a brief comment about the book simply as an intuitive springboard for further investigation. Don't think about it too much; let the next step occur to you.

Your journey will not follow the same path as anyone else's. You may not be ready for certain insights that your friend learned years ago while you already get lessons your friend is still struggling with. That's why we have each other to learn with along the way. Don't be put off by the fact that a book listed here was first published twenty or thirty years ago. Truth doesn't go out of date and a good tool can be useful for many years. Help is all around you, you have but to reach out and claim it for your use.

Bach, Richard. *Illusions: The Adventures of a Reluctant Messiah.* New York: Delacorte, 1977. One of the most philosophically formative books I've ever read. This allegory-as-novel opened my young mind to bigger spiritual truths.

Berthards, Betty. *The Dream Book: Symbols for Self-Understanding.* Petaluma, CA: New Century Publishers, 2001. Explains how to access and interpret your dreams and has a dictionary of dream symbols that makes a great reference to have at your bedside for when you wake up from a dream you want to understand what your subconscious might be working through.

Brennan, Barbara Ann. *Hands of Light: A Guide to Healing through the Human Energy Field.* New York: Bantam, 1988. Presents matter-of fact explanations of esoteric healing phenomena, plus drawings and images that help readers picture how subtle energies might look. A great reference book for healers.

Deida, David. *The Way of the Superior Man.* Boulder, CO: Sounds True, 1997. A personal growth book written for men, it validates men's perspective and experience with explanations that women will also find fascinating.

Edwards, Betty. *The New Drawing on the Right Side of the Brain.* New York: Tarcher, 1999. A great book to help you understand and *practice* using your logical (left brain) and intuitive (right brain) abilities.

Gordon, Richard. *Your Healing Hands: The Polarity Experience.* Berkeley, CA: North Atlantic Books, 2004. A clearly presented book on polarity. This book demystified energetic healing for a whole generation. It gives simple instructions on how to do polarity treatments to realign unbalanced energy throughout the body.

Hay, Louise. *You Can Heal Your Life.* Carlsbad, CA: Hay House, 1984. This useful reference guide lists the possible emotional and psychological issues associated with different parts of the body and/

or various disease patterns. When I come across a pattern I haven't seen before, I consult this list to see if the issue and solution listed makes intuitive sense to me. It is a great jumping off point for further investigation and has great affirmations.

Hendricks, Gay. *Conscious Breathing: Breathwork for Health, Stress Relief and Personal Mastery.* New York: Bantam, 1995. I constantly recommend this book to give people additional support when shifting from shallow to full breathing. Gives detailed information and exercises to open and expand the breath.

Hendrix, Harville. *Getting the Love You Want: A Guide for Couples.* New York: Holt, 1998. This book gives fantastic insight and tools to help you diagnose where and why you get stuck in intimate relationships.

Johnson, Robert A. *Inner Work: Using Dreams and Active Imagination for Personal Growth.* San Francisco: Harper, 1989. I use the ideas from this book as a springboard for doing rituals to release outmoded emotions and behavior patterns.

Kurchinka, Mary Sheedy. *Raising Your Spirited Child: A Guide for Parents Whose Child Is More Intense, Sensitive, Perceptive, Persistent, and Energetic.* New York: Harper, 2006. Helped me understand how and why I had needs that weren't met as a child. I loan my copy to adults with similar patterns and parents with bright and challenging kids.

Liedoff, Jean. *The Continuum Concept*: In Search of Happiness Lost. New York, da Capo Press, 1986. Helped me trust my own instincts and those of my children. We have what we need to survive and thrive.

McMillen, Kim, and Alison McMillen. *When I Loved Myself Enough.* New York: St. Martin's, 2001. This beautiful, sweet little book is full of wisdom and loving encouragement. It's one of those illumined bedside companions you want to revisit often.

Myss, Caroline. *Anatomy of the Spirit: The Seven Stages of Power and Healing.* New York: Three Rivers Press, 1997. This is definitely a mastery-level book for dedicated students of healing. Explores esoteric and deep level reasons for why we face physical challenges.

Peck, M. Scott. *The Road Less Traveled: A New Psychology of Love, Traditional Values and Spiritual Growth.* New York: Simon & Schuster, 1978. Revolutionary when it first came out, this book inspired a whole generation to understand and initiate their own inner/spiritual healing journey. It's full of profound psychological insights without being too "heady."

Phillips, Jan. *Marry Your Muse: Making a Lasting Commitment to Your Creativity.* Wheaton, IL: Quest Books, 1997. Full of encouragement and support to express and fulfill the creative side of yourself.

Rain, Mary Summer. *In Your Dreams: The Ultimate Dream Dictionary.* Charlottesville, VA: Hampton Roads, 1996. Explains how to access and interpret your dreams and has a dictionary of dream symbols that makes a great reference to have at your bedside for when you wake up from a dream you want to understand what your subconscious might be working through.

Sarno, John E. *Healing Back Pain: The Mind-Body Connection.* New York: Warner, 1991. This ground-breaking book introduced the idea that physical pain (especially in the back) is usually a manifestation of emotional blockage and/or imbalance rather than a purely physical phenomenon.

Schnarch, David. *Passionate Marriage: Keeping Love and Intimacy Alive in a Committed Relationship.* New York: Norton, 1997. A wonderful, positive book with psychological and spiritual insights for deepening intimate relationships.

Thomashauer, Regena. *Mama Gena's Owner's and Operator's Guide to Men.* New York: Simon & Schuster, 2004. A must-read if you are a woman ready to open into your more joyful and playful feminine self. Shows you how to take responsibility for your own pleasure in all aspects of life—with men and without.

Tolle, Eckhart. *The Power of Now: A Guide to Spiritual Enlightenment.* Novato, CA: New World Library, 1999. This is a tremendously powerful book about personal transformation through the present moment. I keep a copy by my bed and refer to it continually.

☯